IMAGES
of America

HEMPHILL COUNTY

Shown are the Santa Fe Depot and Harvey House in Canadian, Texas. In a move still regretted by many in Hemphill County, the depot, which anchored Main Street, was demolished in 1976. The Santa Fe Railway had moved its employees from Canadian to Amarillo in 1954, and passenger service was suspended in 1968. (Courtesy of the River Valley Pioneer Museum.)

ON THE COVER: From left to right, the second through fifth men are Tom Berry, W. W. Owens (early hotel operator), W. H. Hopkins (early rancher), and John Black. (Courtesy of the River Valley Pioneer Museum.)

IMAGES
of America

HEMPHILL COUNTY

Susan Caudle and the
River Valley Pioneer Museum

ARCADIA
PUBLISHING

Published by Arcadia Publishing
Charleston SC, Chicago IL, Portsmouth NH, San Francisco CA

Library of Congress Control Number: 2009921913

For all general information contact Arcadia Publishing at:
Telephone 843-853-2070
Fax 843-853-0044
E-mail sales@arcadiapublishing.com
For customer service and orders:
Toll-Free 1-888-313-2665

Visit us on the Internet at www.arcadiapublishing.com

This volume is dedicated to my late parents,
H. L. "Red" and Frances Trenfield Owens,
who gave generously of their time to Hemphill County
and provided me with an enduring heritage that made this effort possible.

CONTENTS

ACKNOWLEDGMENTS

I would like to express my gratitude to the River Valley Pioneer Museum Board of Directors for coauthoring this effort and providing unlimited access to all the photographs in their collection. A special thank-you goes to director Sharon Wright for her support and board members Jacqui Haygood and David Cunningham for their "wordsmith" skills.

Special thanks also go to our "historians"—Gena Tubb, Buddy Hobdy, and Rhea Wilson—for their patience in answering questions and providing an accurate review of all segments. Thanks to Jerry and Chalk for the photographic expeditions.

Many residents reviewed individual segments and captions, and provided photographs from their personal collections; they are thanked for gaps they filled and the special flavor of this effort.

My early love of history can be traced to my grandmother Mabel Trenfield and my sister, Eleanor. The late Hub Hext, my sixth-grade history teacher, and Ronald Barney, my high school history teacher, took that initial interest to new heights and ensured that my love of this subject would last a lifetime.

Unless otherwise noted, all images appear courtesy of the River Valley Pioneer Museum.

Introduction

Hemphill County lies in the northeast part of the Panhandle of Texas. It is bordered on the east by Oklahoma, the west by Roberts County, the south by Wheeler County, and the north by Lipscomb County.

For the 200 years leading up to 1875, nomadic Native American tribes representing the Apache, Comanche, Kiowa, and others roamed the Panhandle following the huge buffalo herds. In the search for an alternate route to California through Santa Fe, Josiah Gregg (1840) and Capt. Randolph Marcy (1845) surveyed trails that crossed Hemphill County, following the south bank of the Canadian River.

The battles of the Red River War of 1875–1876 mark an effort by the U.S. Army to contain the Native American threat in the Panhandle. Before this war, buffalo hunters and Native Americans were the main presence in the Panhandle, but settlers were anxious to safely travel to the rich lands. In September 1874, two major battles of the Red River War occurred in what would become Hemphill County: the Battle of Lyman's Wagon Train and the Battle of Buffalo Wallow. The end of the 12 major engagements of the Red River War saw the awarding of a total of 36 Congressional Medals of Honor, six to the men at Buffalo Wallow. The Red River War was a watershed event for the development of the Panhandle in that the Native American barrier to settlement was broken for the first time.

In the spring of 1875, A. G. Springer, a former buffalo hunter, established a trading post/way station in what would eventually be northeastern Hemphill County. Soldiers from Fort Elliott about 30 miles southwest and other buffalo hunters were his main clientele. He ran several hundred head of cattle and has been identified as establishing the first ranch in the Panhandle. On November 17, 1878, Springer and an associate were killed in a gunfight with buffalo soldiers from Fort Elliott over a poker game. Both were buried at the ranch. Later an army investigation at Fort Elliott resulted in the troopers' acquittal.

On April 12, 1879, Wheeler County became the first organized county in the Panhandle, with 14 other unorganized counties attached to it, one of which was Hemphill County. Hemphill County was organized in July 1887. After 1876, investors began to purchase lands in the county for large-scale ranching. The BarCC Cresswell Ranch, headquartered in Roberts County, came to occupy much of western Hemphill County. In 1878, the Moody-Andrews Land and Cattle Company established its PO Ranch in the western and central sections of the county. By 1880, fourteen ranches with combined herds of about 9,600 cattle had been established. A severe winter in 1886 and heavy losses caused the breakup of the larger syndicates, and smaller ranches and farms began to form.

In 1886, the Southern Kansas Railway Company, a Santa Fe subsidiary, began to build a rail line into the Panhandle. The tracks entered Hemphill County during 1887 and further encouraged settlement in the area. The railroad created three town sites: Mendota, Canadian, and Glazier. Hemphill County was organized and separated from Wheeler County in 1887, with Canadian as the county seat. Canadian was designated a division point by the Santa Fe in 1907, diversifying the principally ranching economy present up to that time. The Santa Fe influence would remain strong until the mid-1950s, when Santa Fe moved its employees to Amarillo.

On July 4, 1888, the first rodeo in Texas, and perhaps the world, was held on Main Street of Canadian, Texas. It began as a competition among some of the larger ranches in the area. According to Carl Studer, "Contestants rode until either the horse or man proved better. These contestants ran the risk of plunging into buildings, railings or spectators." In 1918, J. C. Studer's Anvil Park Ranch sponsored the first professional rodeo that was open to the public. The Anvil Park Ranch Rodeo sponsored events from 1918 through 1944. By 1946, rodeo grandstands were built on land leased from the Santa Fe, and the rodeo tradition continues today on the Fourth of July.

From 1900 to 1919, some of the greatest growth occurred in the county, as evidenced by the number of businesses, homes, and churches that were constructed. Had an aerial photograph been taken in 1910, the view would have included large construction sites at the Moody Hotel, the Hoover Building, the First Baptist Church, the Hoover residence, the J. F. Johnson residence, and the C. H. Shaller residence. These substantial homes joined the existing Tom Jones and John Jones residences, the Brainard residence, the First National Bank, and the recently completed Hemphill County Courthouse. By 1930, crops were grown on 86,000 acres in Hemphill County. The cattle industry remained strong, and in 1930, there were more than 55,000 cattle in the county. The departure of Santa Fe employees in the mid-1950s was expected to be fatal to the county's economy. Residents were determined to prove the prediction wrong.

During the 1970s, the county grew, thanks to a rapid expansion of oil production. Though oil was discovered in the county in 1955, production remained relatively small because the technology had not yet progressed to efficiently capture the deep reserves known to exist. By 1974, oil production had reached 999,000 barrels and more than 1,891,000 barrels in 1978. The oil boom had arrived, and many public buildings were constructed, including a new Canadian High School and Elementary School, the Hemphill County Hospital, and the Canadian High School football stadium. The oil bubble burst in the 1980s. By 2000, about 505,000 barrels of oil and more than 8 billion cubic feet of natural gas were produced in the county, but the future looked bright.

In 2000, the county had 239 farms and ranches covering 546,373 acres, 85 percent of which were devoted to pasture and 15 percent to crops. In that year, farmers and ranchers in the area earned $92,490,000, principally in livestock sales. An emphasis on ecotourism, taking advantage of the incredible landscape and habitat, has diversified the economy of Hemphill County. Farmers and ranchers continue efforts to preserve the land and habitat for future generations.

RESOURCES AND SELECTED READINGS

Harris, Sallie B. *Cowmen and Ladies.* Canyon, TX: Staked Plains Press, 1977.

Hemphill County Preservation Committee. *Hemphill County History.* Dallas, TX: Taylor Publishing, 1985.

Robertson, Pauline, and R. L. Robertson. *Panhandle Pilgrimage.* Amarillo, TX: Paramount Publishing Company, 1978.

Texas State Historical Association, *Handbook of Texas Online:* www.tshaonline.org/handbook/online/. Denton, TX: University of North Texas.

One

HIGH OVER THE FIELDS OF BATTLE

BEFORE 1879

"Aud" surveys the landscape inhabited by her forefathers from a mesa just south of Canadian, Texas, on Highway 83/60. Gene Cockrell created the 50-foot, 1-ton dinosaur and perched her there in 1992. Aud, named for Gene's wife, Audrey, has become an area attraction. Occasionally, she sports a carefully applied coat of black and gold paint, the colors of Canadian High School.

Horace Rivers, shown at left, came to Canadian as a child in 1920. Although his primary occupation was founding and operating the Rivers Glass Shop, he discovered an avocation as an archeologist in the rich breaks of the Canadian River and surrounding ranch land. From Native American artifacts to prehistoric evidence of mastodons and dinosaurs, Rivers's finds intrigue visitors to the River Valley Pioneer Museum, where many of his discoveries are on display.

E. E. Polly came to the Texas Panhandle from Kansas in 1873. He was scouting for a place to establish a business and file on land. Ephraim Polly purchased Triangle ranch land formerly belonging to the BarCC and before that to Joseph Morgan. The dugout, shown above, is located in northern Hemphill County. Ephraim Polly was elected the first judge of Hemphill County in 1887 and also served as postmaster.

In 1874, the U.S. Army began a process of subduing native tribes located in the Texas Panhandle in what has been termed the Red River Wars. In southwestern Hemphill County, the Native Americans crossed the path of a 36-wagon supply train commanded by Capt. Wyllys Lyman, which was rushing to relieve Col. Nelson Miles. The Texas Historical Marker is shown above with a modern-day bullet hole. The Buffalo Wallow monument, shown below, identifies the September 12, 1874, site of a battle, concurrent with Lyman's Wagon Train standoff. Six men fought at Buffalo Wallow with 125 warriors, some of whom had come from the siege of the wagon train. All six American participants were awarded the Congressional Medal of Honor. The Native American threat to settlement ended at the completion of the Red River Wars during which these two battles were fought.

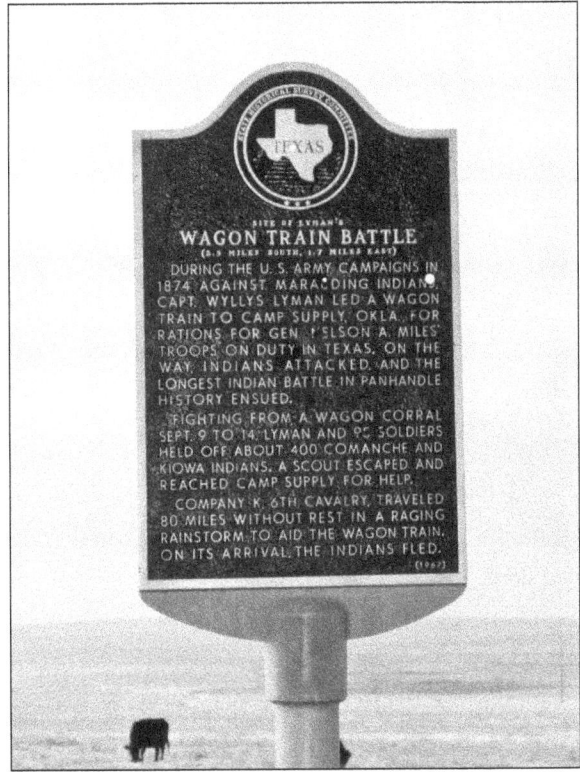

The Springer Ranch was the first ranch in the Texas Panhandle. After the Red River War of 1874, A. G. Springer settled on a parcel of land on Boggy Creek, just north of its junction with the Canadian River. He constructed a dugout with several rooms to serve as a general store, hotel and saloon, and living quarters. Being on the military route between Camp Supply and Fort Elliott, this dugout served as a gathering place for soldiers, travelers, and buffalo hunters. On November 17, 1878, A. G. Springer and Tom Ledbetter were killed in a gunfight with buffalo soldiers over a poker game. A subsequent army investigation at Fort Elliott resulted in the troopers' acquittal. Since the 1940s, part of the roadhouse, shown below, has been covered by Lake Marvin.

Two

BUFFALO HUNTERS AND RANCHING
1880–1899

Samuel Wood, a buffalo hunter, arrived in what would become Hemphill County with his wife, Ellen, in 1874. In 1887, after a nomadic existence hunting buffalo, they homesteaded at Hogtown (above), across the river from what would become Canadian. With George and Sylvania Wood Simpson, they are considered the true pioneer settlers in Hemphill County. Descendants of both families live in Hemphill County today.

Shown above are cowboys associated with the BarCC ranch in 1889. Henry Cresswell founded the BarCC in 1877 along with a syndicate of investors. Its one million acres covered parts of three Panhandle counties, including Hemphill. Many of the early ranchers in the county had their start working for the BarCC, including Ed Brainard, O. R. McMordie, and W. J. Todd. Around 1900, the BarCC closed its operations.

In 1882, the Texas Land and Cattle Company syndicate purchased rights to range land in southeastern Hemphill County. "Bee" Hopkins served as the range foreman for the then-named Laurel Leaf Ranch. In 1888, reverses from land legislation, falling cattle prices, and severe weather compelled the company to sell its Panhandle holdings. Shown above is the Sanders ranch at the site of the former Laurel Leaf headquarters.

In 1888, E. H. "Ed" Brainard's stucco house at 601 Kingman Avenue (shown above) was built as one of the first "town" homes for ranchers needing a second home to accommodate their activities. Ed Brainard came to Texas with the Pollards and Robert Moody in 1882. He went to work for the BarCC, where he continued as foreman until 1895. He founded the Lazy B Ranch, which is still in operation today.

W. J. "Cobb" Conatser came to Hemphill County from Tennessee in 1885 and worked for the Laurel Leaf Ranch. He and Mary Ann Fawcett married in 1896, and in 1905, they moved to the ranch on Boggy Creek. In 1942, the family purchased additional acreage formerly known as the Springer Ranch. Shown above, the house on this property became the main dwelling.

The above seven-gabled residence was built in 1890 on Main Street by Judge Frank Willis. W. J. Todd purchased the home upon the death of Judge Willis in 1894. Shown above from left to right are children Mary, Laura, and William Jr., and parents Laura and Jep Todd. Jep Todd purchased land and moved to the Canadian River area after leaving the BarCC ranch in 1895. His ranch continues in the hands of the Nix family, Laura Todd Nix's descendants. Shown at left is William Dale Nix Sr., who owned and operated the Nix Ranch and Nix Cattle Company for more than 60 years. Dale Nix was chairman of the Texas A&M College of Agriculture Development Council from 1982 to 1983 and owner/ operator of the Nix Ranch/ Cattle Company in Hemphill County for more than 60 years.

Although the above photograph was taken during the Texas-Oklahoma Fair of 1910, it is an accurate depiction of the second Gerlach Store, which was located at Hogtown before the completion of the Santa Fe Railway Bridge across the Canadian River. The first store was actually a dugout on Horse Creek, some 7 miles north of Canadian. Gerlach Mercantile, operated by John and George Gerlach at Third and Main Streets, burned in 1916, and the Gerlach brothers then established the Canadian Hardware Company and Everybody's Dry Goods and Clothing Store. It was said that the Gerlach brothers could "marry a man, build his home, furnish it, supply him with groceries, dry goods, implements, and other necessities of life, and when he no longer had need for them, bury him." Shown below is the Gerlach Mercantile Store from 1910. (Below, courtesy of Jeri Pundt.)

On November 12, 1888, the Rock School (pictured above) opened in Canadian at Fifth Street and Kingman Avenue. Mary Brainard was the teacher, and there were 20 pupils that first year. Brainard said the Native Americans would look in the windows as she taught her classes, grin their approval, and go on. She married Will Isaacs after three years and retired from teaching. Mary Brainard Isaacs served as Women's Christian Temperance Union (WCTU) treasurer and reporter from 1904 to 1948. Shown below is one of the early classes attending the Rock School.

In 1888, the First Presbyterian Church was organized under the direction of Rev. Thomas Dearing. The church was built by subscription from and used by all denominations. This photograph depicts the 1948 building at Sixth and Purcell Streets, but the church bell was purchased in 1890.

Seven women chartered the First Baptist Church in 1894. Those women were Sallie Arrington, Mattie Gallagher, Mrs. J. T. Jackson, Elizabeth Johnson, Mrs. Walter Lyon, Susan Stickley, and Ella Studer. The building, shown above, was constructed in 1910. It served the Baptist congregation until 1954, when a new church was built at Seventh and Main Streets on land given to the church by Dora Gerlach.

Capt. George "Cap" Arrington (seated, left) is shown above with his extended family. He served in the Civil War as a scout in Mosby's Raiders, as a Texas Ranger, where he earned the "captain" title. Later he became sheriff in Wheeler County and then Hemphill County. The house shown below was a "Van Tien" prefabricated home shipped from Iowa to Canadian and assembled in 1919. French Arrington, third from the left in the second row, succeeded "Cap" Arrington as manager. Today the ranch is under the management of the Arrington family. The house and the intersection near it were featured at the beginning and end of the movie *Castaway*.

The First Methodist Church was organized in 1894, and the first church building was completed in 1903. The current structure was completed in 1929 and was renovated and expanded several times during the next 60 years. One of the later remodels is shown here. The church recognizes the commitment of early congregants, including George Addison, W. C. Teague, Jim Strader, George Tubb, H. M. Petree, Mrs. Spiller, Mabel Teas, and many others.

In 1909, the First Christian Church was founded, meeting initially in the Opera House. The white frame courthouse was replaced by the current stone courthouse in 1909. The church purchased the wood courthouse in 1910 and moved it to the location of Fourth and Purcell Streets. It served as the church until 1914, when the redbrick church (shown above) was built on the same site.

In 1895, the Opera House was built on Main Street to provide a meeting place for the Independent Order of Odd Fellows (IOOF) and Rebekahs. IOOF is a fraternal service organization, and the Rebekah Lodge is the ladies' branch. Ben Tepe completed the construction of this 30-by-70-foot frame building in 90 days. Overflow parking was available at the wagon yard at Third Street and Kingman Avenue. Many organizations and churches used the ground floor for meetings. Although not shown in the photograph above, the original building was white with a red roof. Local talent, including H. E. Hoover and D. J. Young, participated in plays. Chautauqua events brought entertainment and culture for the whole community. Shown below is one of the curtains used for the stage with advertisements for local establishments.

The Canadian Band varied in size in its early years. Among those pictured are, in no particular order, Walter Teague (leader and music director), Harry Cornelius, R. M. Hibbard, Homer and Flora Marks, Ed Bader, Perry Hazelwood, and Harold Reed. In 1904, J. C. Studer, A.V. McQuiddy, R. H. Stone, Layne Addison, George Jamison, and J. E. Corson were included in the roster that marched in parades and appeared in other towns.

Charles Stickley came to Canadian in 1900 and worked on his uncle Vas Stickley's ranch. He had attended an embalming school and was available in 1902 with the necessary skills when a cowboy drowned in the Canadian River. The cowboy's family wanted him embalmed and shipped to Wichita, Kansas. Gerlach's store provided the chemicals, and Charles prepared the body for shipment. His funeral business began with this event.

J. C. Studer came to the Panhandle at the age of 24 from Switzerland. By 1887, he arrived in Canadian as a buffalo hunter, gunsmith, and blacksmith. He opened a livery stable and bought land that became the Anvil Park Ranch, shown above. In 1950, he sold 5,000 acres of the Anvil Park Ranch to the State of Texas for a wildlife refuge. The Gene Howe Wildlife Management Area exists today.

Temple Houston was the last child of Republic of Texas president Sam Houston. He served as district attorney in 1882, in the 35th Judicial District, which covered the Texas Panhandle. After serving as a state senator, he returned to the Panhandle as an attorney for the railroad and lived in Canadian in the house shown above. He later moved to Woodward, Indian Territory, where he died in 1905.

24

Shown above is the ranch currently known as Indian Mound Ranch, located on the Gageby Creek, which was homesteaded in 1890 by Ed and Leuna George, pictured at right with their four oldest children in 1896. Ed came to the Panhandle in 1879. Leuna's father came as a buffalo hunter in 1878. They married in 1886 and raised nine children. In the early days, Native Americans would walk up the creek from Oklahoma, come to the ranch house, and peer into the windows; however, the ranch was never attacked. Several George descendants still ranch on the original George land, with additional land added. Lee George's daughter, Gayle, and her husband, Wayne Haygood, moved their Indian Mound Ranch Herefords here in 1981. Lee and Jacqui Haygood and sons are currently running Indian Mound Ranch with both Hereford and Angus purebred cattle, and commercial cows. (Both, courtesy of the Haygood family and Indian Mound Ranch.)

25

Shown above is the present Edith Ford Memorial Cemetery, which was founded in 1908. The McGee addition was named for Tom McGee, the first sheriff of Hemphill County, who was murdered in 1894. During the next 100 years, two more officers—Corky Guthrie and Jim Bruce Graham—would join McGee as having lost their lives in the line of duty. Brainard/Isaacs and more Edith Ford additions would later increase the initial cemetery size.

Shown above is the Canadian Athletic Club championship baseball team from 1906. This team competed regionally within the 31st Judicial District. Many notables served on this team, including Tom Hoover, center field, and Bruce Waterfield, mascot. Much later, Waterfield would marry Marjorie Jones, daughter of Tom Jones, and have two sons, James and Richard. The Waterfield family continues a ranching tradition today.

Three

BOOM AND THE
SANTA FE RAILROAD
1900–1909

The photograph shown above illustrates the construction of the first Santa Fe Railway Bridge across the Canadian River. The first bridge was built near the Clear Creek settlement but had to be moved in 1908 because of structural concerns caused by the weight of the trains.

Santa Fe Station and Eating House.   CANADIAN, Texas.

The Santa Fe Depot and Harvey House, shown above, were completed in 1906 at a cost of $35,000. Fred Harvey was contracted with the Santa Fe to build eating places along the rail line. He advertised for "Harvey Girls" who were of good moral character, had at least an eighth-grade education, displayed good manners, and were neat and articulate. These women brought respectability to waitressing and conformed to Fred Harvey's rigid rules by not dating for the length of their contract. Several Harvey Girls from the Canadian location married and settled down in Hemphill County. Below is a unique picture of Canadian's Harvey Girls. Fred Harvey did not allow pictures to be taken of people in his dining rooms, but this one was taken by Julius Born, an early Hemphill County photographer.

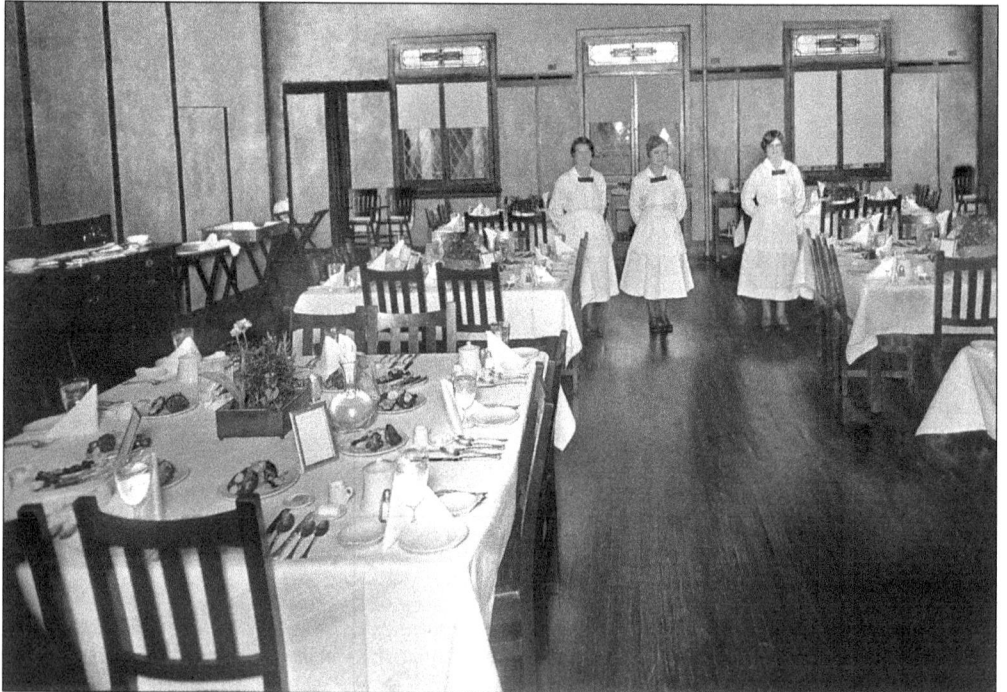

After the brick Santa Fe Depot and Harvey House were completed, work began on the roundhouse, a large semicircular structure, in 1907. The turntable at the roundhouse was used to either switch engines or to rotate the engine in a different direction. Shown above, the roundhouse at Canadian was completed in 1908. Unfortunately, it was consumed by fire shortly after it opened. It was rebuilt and served for many years.

Shown above, the Santa Fe Reading Room was built at a cost of $25,000 by 1908. The reading room provided a number of sleeping apartments available to railroad employees. It was arranged so that public rooms could be combined to support concerts, plays, and traveling shows that were provided by the rail line. Local townspeople were welcome and did attend the free events sponsored by Santa Fe.

The photograph above shows Julius Born's variety store on Main Street. Seated in front of the store are, from left to right, James Hartnett, Walter Cain, and an unidentified man. Julius Born came to Canadian in 1897, and this store, opened in 1905, was one of his first business ventures. He bottled and sold sarsaparilla and carried many other items, but his real legacy lay in the photographs he took of early Panhandle residents and businesses. Thanks to Juhree Carr's salvage of the glass negatives after Born's death in the 1960s, the River Valley Pioneer Museum preserved and digitized the almost 5,000 negatives. Several of the photographs in this book are from his original negatives. The photograph at left is one Born took of possibly his own camera and a lovely child who was looking through it. As with most of his negatives, no name is associated with this child.

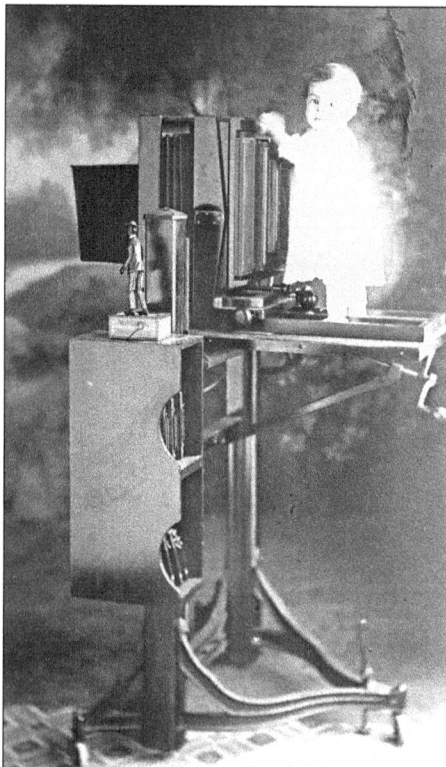

In 1905, Frank Jamison purchased the *Canadian Record* from the founder and first publisher, W. S. Definbaugh. Jamison and his wife, shown at right, remained in Canadian until 1919. Showing humor, skill, and style throughout his tenure, Jamison wrote of the July 4, 1905, parade as follows: "We are not able to report the donkey race, because they haven't reached the mark as we go to press."

By 1948, Ben and Nancy Ezzell (shown at left) joined the *Canadian Record* newspaper and, by 1949, fully owned the newspaper. Much of the community's history is documented in the archives of the *Canadian Record*, maintained by the Hemphill County Public Library. The writing in the newspaper is a regular award winner in state and national contests. The Ezzell tradition continues, with Laurie Ezzell Brown serving as the editor since 1993. (Courtesy of Laurie Ezzell Brown.)

The Academy, shown above, opened its doors in September 1904 on Sixth Street. It was formed under the trusteeship of H. E. Hoover, D. J. Young, J. A. Chambers, J. F. Johnson, and George Gerlach. It offered elementary, high school, and college credit. In 1904, there were four teachers and 27 students. By the next year, enrollment increased to 117. In 1910, a bond issue of $25,000 was passed for the construction of the first public high school. By 1913, the high school graduated 12 students while the Academy only had four graduates. This was its final year of operation. The Academy's contribution to early Hemphill County education was important. Many future teachers and civic leaders were taught there, including John Young, Mary and Laura Todd, Mabel Addison, Carl and Floyd Studer, and Tom and Ed Hoover.

The Academy's girls' dormitory (pictured above) was built in 1906–1907 at Sixth Street and Cheyenne Avenue at a cost of $6,000. According to *The Student*, the Academy yearbook, "The two-story building nearly encircled by a long arched veranda is equipped with a hot air heating system, hot and cold water system, bath and toilet." Under watchful care, boarders "will not be found on the streets or out at night, but will be at their books." Boarding students were also required to attend study hall on weeknights from 7:00 to 9:30 p.m. Board was $14 per month. The boys' and girls' dormitory sites were advertised as "private and secluded." The boys' dormitory is shown below.

John Jones came to the Panhandle with his brother Tom in 1883 and purchased land on the south side of the Canadian River. Shown above is the home built at 406 North Sixth Street with cast-stone blocks made in his front yard. The Stickley brothers built this house along with many other homes in Canadian. John Jones's land is in the hands of the McMordie family today.

Thomas Jones constructed the first brick residence in Canadian in 1909 at Main and Sixth Streets, as shown above. Thomas and his brother, John, came to Canadian in 1883, later dividing the ranch between the two of them. Thomas and his wife, Rosalie, had three children: Thomas Stanley Jones II, Gwenfred Jones Chambers, and Marjorie Jones Waterfield. Descendants of Thomas Jones continue the ranching tradition today.

J. F. Johnson entered the merchandising business in Kansas, Oklahoma, and Texas. One of his earlier stores was constructed in Higgins, Texas, in 1887. Once the Santa Fe crossed the Canadian River, he built the store (shown above) at Fourth and Main Streets in Canadian. He was active in all civic affairs and involved in banking, ranching, and cattle.

The photograph above shows a Johnson Mercantile Delivery wagon apparently receiving some assistance with its harness. In the background is a feed store with advertising on the side touting a minstrel show occurring at the Opera House in Canadian.

The county was organized in 1886 with the presentation of a petition of 49 signatures requesting to be detached from Wheeler County. Judge Frank Willis was the district judge presiding in late 1887 over a court comprised of, among others, Tom McGee, sheriff; B. M. Baker, attorney; E. E. Polly, county judge; and Hoose Hopkins, the district and county clerk. The first courthouse, a tent, was quickly replaced by a wooden structure in 1887. This structure served until it was replaced by the current stone structure in 1909. In the photograph above, construction is underway for the stone courthouse, and below is the image of the completed courthouse, which is still in use today.

John Chambers worked as a wrangler on the Springer Ranch in 1883. Once the railroad came to Canadian, Chambers opened a mercantile store (pictured above) with Mose Hays, whom he later bought out. When Myrtle Winsett came to Canadian following her sisters, Elizabeth Johnson and Jane Bragg Hoover, John took notice and soon married her. Her brother, James Winsett, joined in partnership with the store. The Chambers store operated in Canadian until 1928. Shown below is the interior of the Chambers store, so typical of mercantile stores of the time. The treadle sewing machine seen in the center aisle, umbrellas, hat, and boxes at upper right, and rolls of fabric are a few of the many items available to the early client.

The Canadian Valley Bank was founded in 1892 with Robert Moody as president and D. J. Young as cashier. The bank was chartered in 1903, and a building at Third and Main Streets was constructed in 1907. The current bank building, at Second and Main Streets as shown above, absorbed some of the earlier banks, including the Isaacs-Brainard Bank (1937) and J. F. Johnson's Southwest National Bank (1939).

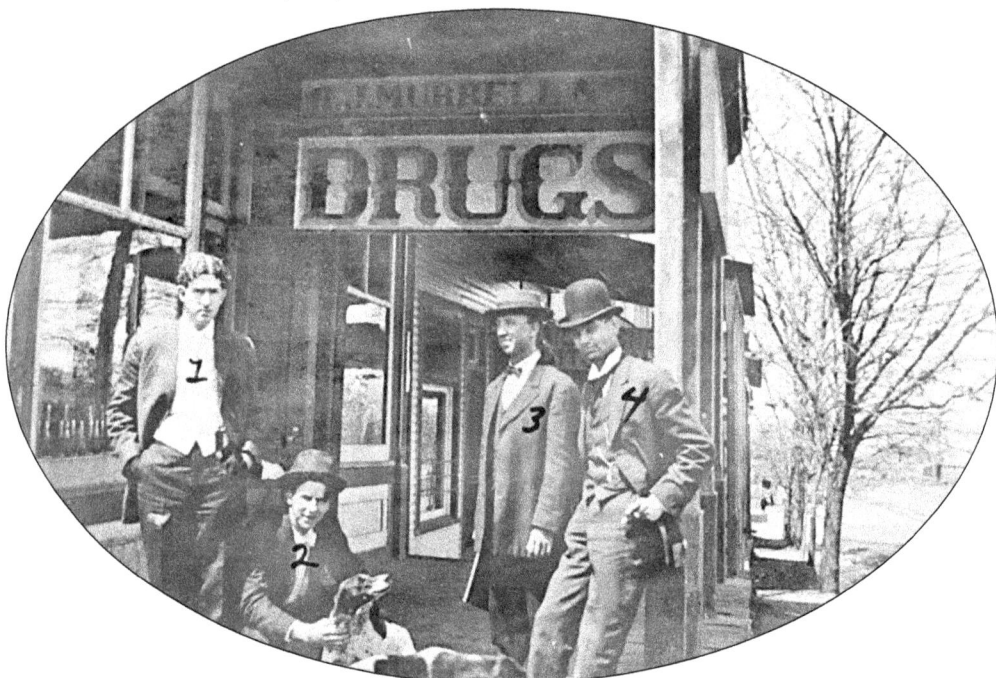

Shown above is a photograph of a Dr. Francis Teas and a Dr. Harvey Caylor (noted with Nos. 3 and 4, respectively). Dr. Caylor founded the first hospital in Canadian in 1917, and Dr. Teas came to Canadian in the early 1900s. He courted the widow Mabel Owens Waterfield for many years, but she refused to marry until she had seen her son Bruce graduate from college. Her grandsons, Jim and Dick Waterfield, continued the ranching tradition established by their grandfather.

Some of Hemphill County's first establishments were saloons. They would have prospered with or without the railway expansion; however, they grew considerably in number with the advent of the railway. The Women's Christian Temperance Union (WCTU), founded in 1902, worked diligently to ensure the county voted "dry" in the 1903 referendum on the issue. They succeeded, and the county is still dry today, prohibiting the sale of alcoholic beverages.

W. C. T. U. Building.
Canadian, Texas.

Although the WCTU formed in 1902, it was not until 1911 that their building (shown above) was completed by the Stickleys. The WCTU was instrumental in establishing events such as the first Memorial Day celebration and a cemetery organization. The building now houses the Hemphill County Library and regular Rotary Club meetings, and plays host to the annual bazaar, begun in 1906 to support the building and the library. The building was deeded to the county in the 1980s.

Ben Tepe purchased a lumber company owned by John R. Wright from Cecelia, John's widow, in 1898. The Tepe-Hoover Lumber Company, shown above with a Corson's delivery wagon, was the successor to the B. F. Tepe Lumber Company. The Tepe-Hoover Lumber Company became White House Lumber and later Modern Lumber at the same site on Third Street and Kingman Avenue. The Ben Tepe home, shown below, at Fifth Street and Kingman Avenue, was built in 1916 for his wife, Mary, and four children, twins Vera and Velma, Clifford, and Opal. A ranch in Gem City was run by Benny Tepe, son of Opal, and is in the family today.

RISE IN CANADIAN RIVER
SEPT. 8" 09
CANADIAN   TEXAS

COPYRIGHTED 1909
BY G. A. ADDISON
CANADIAN   TEXAS

George Addison took the above picture of a flooding Canadian River in 1909. He had been the official Fort Sill (Oklahoma Indian Territory) photographer during the time of Chief Quanah Parker and Geronimo in the early 1890s. His amazing pictorial chronicle of the American Indian of this period can be seen at the National Cowboy and Western Heritage Museum in Oklahoma City. While at Fort Sill, family lore indicates he and his wife, Anna Virginia, adopted a two-year-old white captive. This child was named Mabel, and she lived with the family in Canadian. Shown at right is a photograph taken by Julius Born of a 16-year-old Mabel, who would become Mabel Addison Bowen and would teach for several decades in neighboring Ochiltree County.

Robert Moody's house in Long Beach, California, is shown above with members of his family. On the far left are D. J. and Mamie Moody Young. Directly behind them on the steps at the left are Robert Allen and Ada May Moody, followed by E. K. Thurmond and Pearl Moody. Thomas and Gem Hibbard Moody are standing behind and to the right of Robert Moody (standing center). The remaining members of the family on the steps are Edwin and Eva Moody McKinney and John and Maggie Moody Gerlach at front right. The woman seated on the porch is unidentified. Along with banking and real estate interests, Robert Moody built the Moody Hotel, shown below, in 1906 on Main and Second Streets. Below is the showplace and "first fireproof hotel in the Panhandle."

Four

COMMUNITY AND CULTURE
1910–1919

In a photograph from the Anvil Park Rodeo in the 1940s, Bud Dolcater, standing on the right, is helping the other men in the act of "earring down" the horse while attempting to saddle him. One horse has partially leaped over a second horse. Bud was the son of Mae Tubb Dolcater and Henry Donald Dolcator and was a known saddle maker in the area. (Courtesy of Gena Tubb.)

According to lore, the first rodeo in the world was held on Canadian's Main Street on July 4, 1888, as a contest between local ranches. Temple Houston, son of Republic of Texas president Sam Houston, delivered an address. According to Carl Studer, "Lining the streets of the cow town stood hundreds of spectators watching the cowboys . . . risk the peril of attempted conquest of infuriated outlaw horses." This contest was the predecessor of the 1918 Anvil Park Rodeo, founded by Carl Studer's father, J. C. Studer. He wanted to thank the ranches and cowboys who had made his blacksmith and livery business a success. The Anvil Park Ranch was the site of the rodeo from 1918 to 1945 and was attended by cowboys from Canada and all over the United States. The postcard below illustrates saddle bronco riding during this time.

The first lots in the town of Canadian were sold on the Fourth of July in 1888. This began a tradition of annual Fourth of July events that are a highlight of each year in Hemphill County. Shown above is a float in the Fourth of July parade of 1910 on Main Street in front of the Tubb Building. A typical parade included entries from neighboring cities and fire departments, bands, and local organizations. The parade, the annual rodeo, fireworks, and the Old Timer's Bar-B-Que attract visitors from across the United States and ensure that all ages will have a grand time. Shown below is a post parade gathering from the 1920s in front of the Palace Theater and other Main Street buildings.

This 1910 view of Main Street of Canadian, shown above, emphasizes the width of this central and important street. The Santa Fe Depot anchors Main Street with the Hoover Building (foreground left) and the original First National Bank's first building (foreground right) serving as bookends. In the background is Red Deer Creek just before it merges with the Canadian River.

In 1914, the Sacred Heart Catholic Church, shown in the above photograph, was built and became a mission church of Pampa. Subsequent additions have remained true to the simple style of the original church. An early priest for this church, Father Stanley (Stanley F. L. Crocchiola), wrote extensively, including *Rodeo Town*, a book that chronicles early Hemphill County history.

H. E. Hoover had law offices on the second story of the Hoover Building, shown above. The building contained a drugstore, which was operated by J. J. Jennings in the earlier years. A soda fountain has been a permanent fixture in the building since its construction in 1910 and exists today.

Red Kansas bricks were used by H. E. Hoover to build this house at 215 South Fifth Street in 1910. Directly across on Fifth Street, J. F. Johnson, his brother-in-law, was building his house, and the First Baptist Church was being built a block away. Hoover became a solicitor for Santa Fe in 1892 and was involved in banking and educational development as well as being a renowned attorney.

Four generations of the H. E. Hoover family are shown in the above photograph. H. E. Hoover's mother is seated on the left, young Bobby is standing with his hand on his grandfather's lap, H. E. Hoover is seated on the right, and in the back is Dan, son of H. E. Hoover. H. E. became president of the First National Bank in Canadian and was a partner in the Tepe-Hoover Lumber Company. His fame as an attorney grew nationwide when it became known that he had never lost a case, and his sons Dan and Edgar eventually became his associates in the Hoover-Hoover-Cussens law firm in Canadian. H. E. Hoover was involved in organizing the Panhandle-Plains Historical Society in Canyon, Texas, and served as its president from 1933 to 1935. He purchased a ranch, shown below, and created modern farms by 1931.

Shown above in 1910 at 216 South Fifth Street, J. F. Johnson built a home the Texas Historical Commission has cited as the most outstanding example of the homes built in this era. Early Canadian was influenced by J. F. Johnson in many ways: Johnson Mercantile (1888), Stock Exchange Bank (1902), Southwest National Bank (1921), and as a rancher. Elizabeth Johnson was a founder and president of the WCTU and an accomplished artist.

Charles Henry Shaller and his wife, Ida, arrived in Canadian in 1887 before the Santa Fe Railroad completed construction of the bridge. Charles Shaller purchased land in 1889, and the first family headquarters was located 2 miles east of Canadian. In 1910, the Shaller family moved into the home, shown above, which was built by C. H. Shaller at 1022 Main Street. The Shallers had 11 children, nine of whom survived to adulthood.

The 1918 Canadian High School boys' basketball team is shown at left. The influenza epidemic shortened the 1917 school year, and *The Beargrass* yearbook was issued for both 1917 and 1918. The only break in yearbook publishing occurred from 1932 to 1942 because of the Depression and World War II. Shown below is the 1918 Canadian High School baseball team.

In 1907, the public Rock School was replaced by the Mary Brainard Isaacs School located at Main and Ninth Streets. The Isaacs School remained an elementary school once a high school was funded in 1910. Shown above is the 1910 high school located on the same block as the Rock School at Fifth Street and Kingman Avenue.

Walter Teague, shown above with a mustache, sits in an early (if not the first) hose truck owned by the Canadian Volunteer Fire Department. He was a member of the fire department for 39 years and worked with officials to obtain better equipment and an extension of the water mains. He and his son Lawrence were plumbers by trade.

The Parsell family came to the Panhandle in 1880 and ranched in Roberts County. In 1911, they built their "town" home, shown above, including a ballroom on the third floor. Isabel Parsell was the mother of 13 children, four of whom died young. Their son Hugh Parsell managed the ranch for the family. This home is now owned by the J. B. Reid family.

Vas Stickley came to Canadian in 1887, served as a deputy to Sheriff Tom McGee, and operated a livery stable with Dick Bussell from 1887 to 1893. Harry Stickley, who later constructed many buildings throughout Canadian, came to the area to work on his uncle Vas's ranch. Harry and his brother, Charles, built the house shown above for Vas Stickley at 602 Santa Fe Avenue.

RESIDANCE, CANADIAN, TEX'S.

The Stone house was built in 1916 at 414 North Sixth Street of Kansas bricks. One of the most notable people to be raised in this house was Marion Stone Karr, who attended the Academy and returned to Canadian at the death of her husband in 1939. She ultimately taught English for two generations of Canadian High School students and made instruction entertaining, challenging, and memorable. Shown at right is a photograph from her days as a Canadian High School basketball player in 1918.

Shown above is the Dr. E. H. Snyder residence on Main Street in Canadian. Nona Alexander Snyder was raised in Wheeler and Hemphill Counties, and met Dr. Snyder while attending college in Missouri. After marrying and living in Ohio, they moved to Canadian in 1909. Their children were Helen, Rush, Ruth, and Marjorie; the latter three continued the physician heritage established by Dr. E. H. Snyder. Dr. Rush practiced with his father in Canadian, where he and his wife, Rachel, had three children, Nona Dale, Rush Jr., and Edward, all of whom became doctors. Below is a photograph of the Snyder Clinic on Main Street.

In January 1892, William Isaacs married Mary K. Brainard, Canadian's first schoolteacher and the sister of rancher Edward H. Brainard. In 1893, William and his brother, Sam, purchased a 30,000-acre ranch and 4,000 cattle, establishing their Circle and a Half brand. The above residence, built in 1916 on Kingman Avenue, served as a boardinghouse for single teachers for many years and boasted a lavatory in each bedroom.

Sam Isaacs served as a director of the Canadian Building and Loan Association and helped establish Canadian's Masonic Lodge. The Stickley brothers built his two-story home, shown above, in 1916 at 804 Main Street. Sam Isaacs was a charter member of the Panhandle-Plains Historical Society and was one of the founders of the Panhandle-Plains Historical Museum at Canyon, Texas. He and his brother, Will, established a ranch that is operating today.

Forling the Rive at canadian 7-

John Wood had a horse named Bob, for his bobbed tail, and was noted for "dancing" in place if he was getting mired down in quicksand. This caused the sand to pack until he could move on. According to Sallie Harris in *Cowmen and Ladies*, "Bob could find a safe place to cross when his rider could not be sure." Shown above is a photograph of "fording the Canadian River."

In 1913, Frank Young Sr. expanded his existing ranch by purchasing the headwaters of the Washita River in southwest Hemphill County. His son, Henry Frye Young (shown at left), built a home on the ranch in 1934. Lee, Henry's son, and his two sons have ensured the tradition continues through four generations. A granite cornerstone marking the 1874 camp headquarters of Gen. Nelson Miles is also located on the ranch. (Courtesy of Lee and Genise Young.)

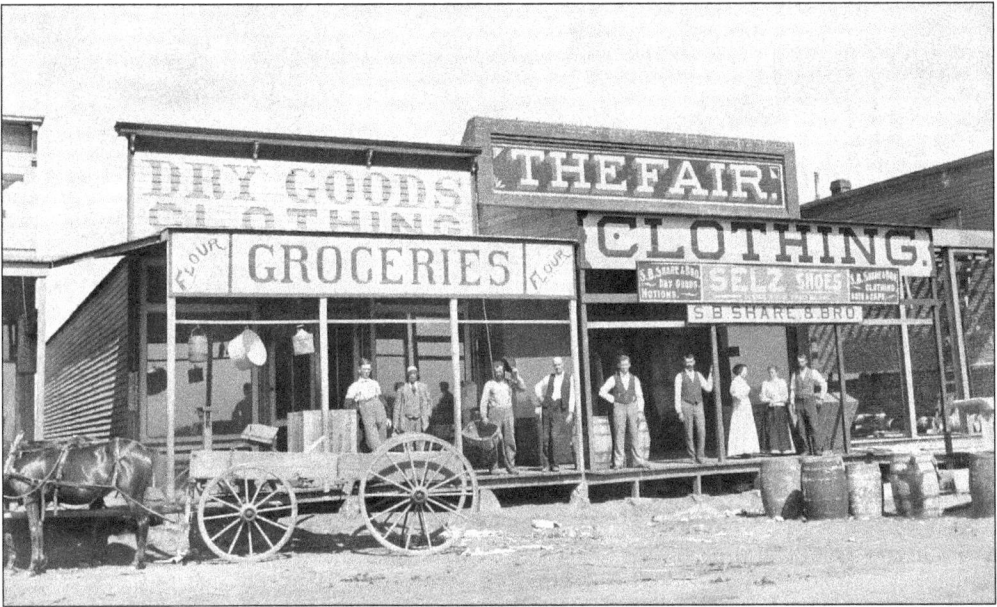

In August 1913, Nahim Abraham opened the Fair Store (shown above) in Canadian. Shortly after the opening, his wife, Alia, and sons Naceeb and Tom came via Ellis Island from Kafaracab, Persia (now Lebanon). This original location was across the street from the Main Street site they moved to in 1917. The interior of the 1917 "second store" is shown below. They would remain at this location, with additions, for the next 50-plus years and close in 1972. With the addition of two more sons, Malouf "Oofie" and Edward, there began a continuing legacy of Abraham civic involvement, preservation of historic sites, and philanthropic support from this family, whose fourth generation is active today. (Both, courtesy of Kay Abraham Brown.)

The above photograph from around 1913 shows Alia Abraham in the foreground (right). She was active in the business and, according to her son Tom, provided meals to Frank "Toppy" Clark, the only black man living in Canadian at the time. She later provided for his burial when he passed away in 1922. (Courtesy of Kay Abraham Brown.)

J. C. Studers had six sons and one daughter. Four of the sons joined the military during World War I. From left to right are (seated) Oscar in the navy uniform and Carl in the cavalry uniform; (standing) Floyd; Otto in the army uniform; J. C. Studer, the boys' father; and John in the air force uniform. Many Hemphill County families made such contributions to the war effort.

Floods of the Canadian River adversely impacted commerce and frequent mention of the need for a wagon bridge can be found in the early *Canadian Record* issues. Finally, in 1916, a bridge (pictured above) spanning 2,635 feet was constructed. At the time, it was the largest steel structure west of the Mississippi River. It remained in service until it was replaced in 1953.

In 1918, the process to build the Dallas-Denver Highway reached in Hemphill County. In the local press, it was appropriately referred to as the Dallas-Canadian-Denver Highway (now U.S. 83) and offered a much needed north-south link for the Panhandle of Texas. Shown above is work occurring in Hemphill County during its construction. The highway was completed in 1921. In the 1940s and 1950s, this major route was paved.

George Addison took this photograph on August 5, 1912. No special mention of this event is made in the *Canadian Record* issues of that time, so it is unknown why the congregation of mules occurred. Notice, from left to right, R. M. Hibbard's Repair Shop, Julius Born's Kandy Kitchen, Jones Hardware, and the First National Bank buildings.

Julius Born (1879–1962), shown at left, remained in Canadian until the end of his days. He and his brother Frederick, who was killed in a saloon fight in 1901, are buried in Edith Ford Memorial Cemetery. His contribution to Hemphill County history through his many photographs cannot be overstated. These glass negatives would have been lost forever had Juhree Carr not rescued them as the store was being torn down.

CANADIAN'S FIRST HOSPITAL

The first hospital in Hemphill County, shown in the above photograph, was built by Dr. H. C. Caylor in 1917 at 213 North Seventh Street. Dr. Caylor eventually moved to Ruidoso, New Mexico, selling the hospital to Dr. E. H. Morris in the early 1920s. Dr. Morris remained in Canadian as one of the two principal doctors, along with Dr. E. H. Snyder and later Dr. Rush Snyder. Their work in the county extended more than 50 years. As a result of the 1947 tornado in Glazier, 260 citizens were treated in this hospital and at the First Methodist Church. Shown below is a photograph of one of the hospital's wards.

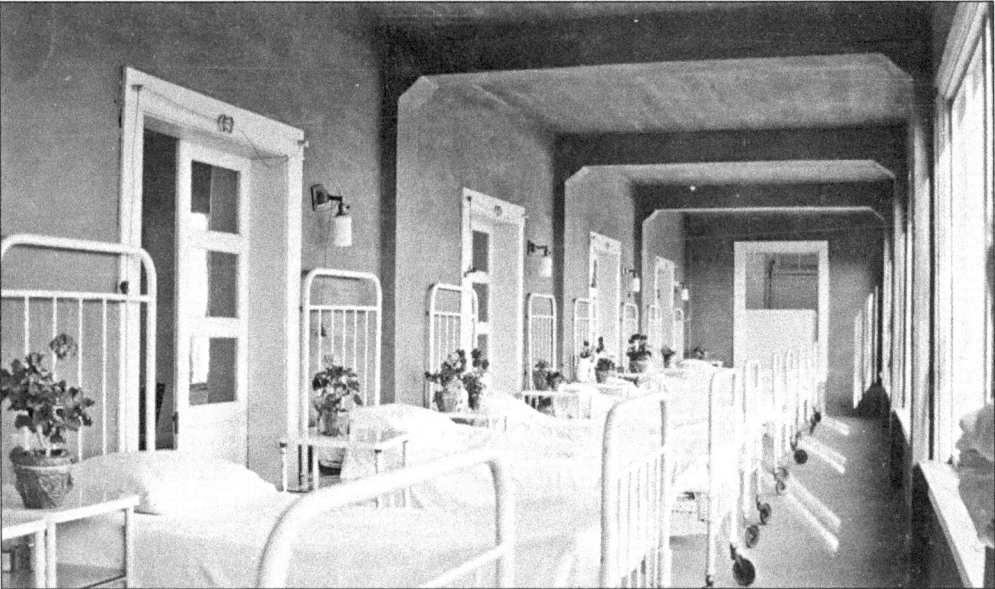

Earl Rhea Sr. (shown at left) served in the U.S. Navy during World War I. He was stationed in Bremerton Naval Station in Washington state and the Great Lakes Naval Station in Chicago. The picture was taken in 1917. He is representative of Hemphill County's sons serving in World War I.

Shown at right is a photograph of W. A. Donaldson and his son Millard. W. A. and Eliza Jane Donaldson moved to the Cataline community in 1889, where they raised their seven children, including Millard, who was born in 1892 and served in World War I.

Five

WE OUR BEST MUST DO
1920–1939

"Black Sunday" was the name given to the darkest, heaviest storm of the "Dust Bowl," which occurred on April 14, 1935. This storm, shown above, affected 100 million acres of the Panhandles of Texas, Oklahoma, and adjoining states. The storm covered an area 200 miles wide with wind speeds as high as 60 miles per hour. The few crops surviving the previous dust storms were wiped out by this single devastating storm.

In the spring and again in the fall of 1923, heavy rains caused damage to the rail bridge, as shown above. This was the first substantial damage to the bridge in 15 years and was caused by logs and debris lodging against the structure. Repairs were made quickly and service restored. The repaired bridge was again upgraded in 1924 to accommodate the increased tonnage of the outgoing freight demand. Shown below is a 1926 view of both the rail bridge at center and the wagon bridge to the right. The wagon bridge had not been damaged in the flood.

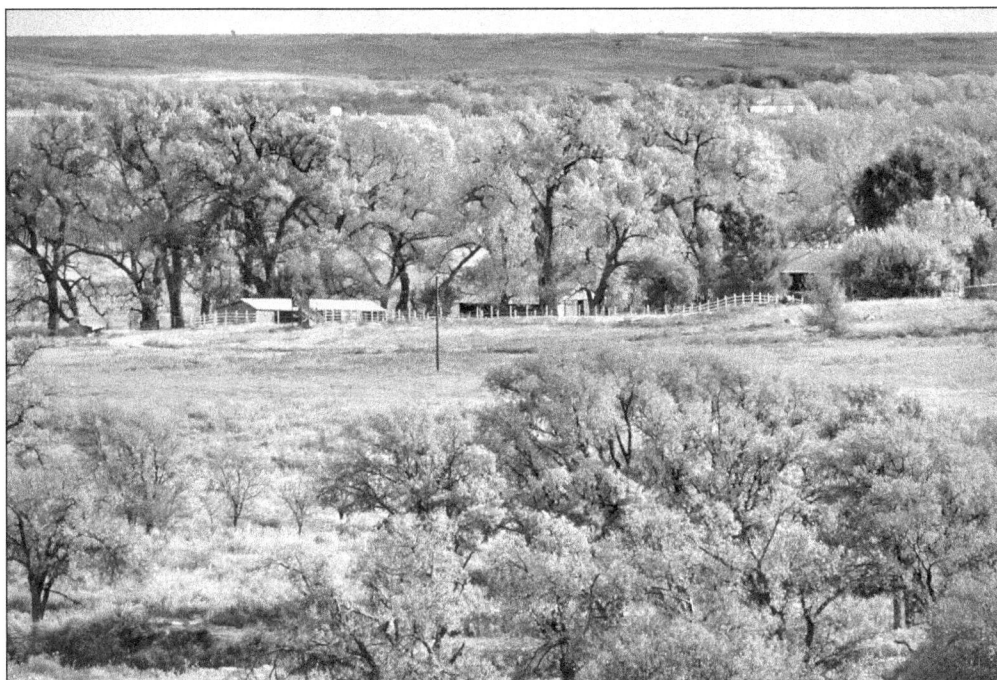

Cecelia Wright, a young widow, sold her husband John R.'s interests in various ventures. With the money, she purchased cattle from her brothers, John and Tom Jones. Wiley Wright and his brothers, sons of Cecelia, had worked on the BarCC while young men in the early 1900s. Entering cattle and ranching themselves, Wiley Wright purchased land from the C. H. Shaller heirs in 1927. Shown above is the Wright Ranch, where he built corrals and had the first set of cattle scales, used by cattlemen from around the region. He and his wife, Lucille, had one child, Charles, who inherited the ranch when Wiley died unexpectedly in 1938. Shown below is a photograph of Charles (far left) and his father, Wiley (far right). The Wright ranch continues today in the hands of third- and fourth-generation descendants.

The Canadian High School basketball team of 1928 is shown above on the only court. Their success was much better than would be expected since the court was outdoors. The team, coached by R. L. Patrick, included Ben Merry, Errol Flathers, Austin Caldwell, Halley Pundt, Albert Boyd, Clark and Harold Sherman, and George Carver.

1928

EARL DODD
CLARENCE WALSER
CLAUDE WITCHER
AUSTIN SHELTON
ELIZABETH HARTNETT
LILLIAN COOK
DAISY COOK
MILDRED WEHRS
LEOLA FILLINGIM
ROBERT ESTES

HAZEL CROWELL
MAY BELLE MURRAY
EVALINE HARDIN
MALOUF ABRAHAM
OLA MAE RUSHING
GEORGE ARCHER
GENE MUSE
HARRY WILBUR
CAROLYN RUTTER
CHARLIE ARCHER

Shown at left is the sophomore class of 1928 standing in front of the 1910 Canadian High School. Future Canadian First National Bank president Harry Wilbur is shown, as is future state representative and entrepreneur Malouf "Oofie" Abraham. Oofie is the first student on the left, first row. Exact names and placement of the other students are not known.

Shown above, Canadian's city hall was built in 1929. The building has served as an early firehouse, the location for city offices, the site of the annual Halloween Carnival, and the annual gathering place for the Old Timer's Reunion and Bar-B-Que on the Fourth of July.

This is the 1924 Fourth of July parade on Main Street. This view represents the 400 block in the foreground, headed north to the Santa Fe Depot at the foot of Main Street. In an event that continues today, the annual parade, the rodeo, fireworks, and the Old Timer's Bar-B-Que attract visitors from across the United States and ensure an exciting time is had by all ages.

The view shown above is one of the few photographs on U.S. Highway 60/83 in Canadian. The courthouse is visible with the rounded dome in the background, with the Opera House across the street to the left. To the right of the courthouse is the First Christian Church. In the foreground, a 1940s vintage school bus is refueling at the Phillips 66 station, and a corner of the Hobdy Motor Company is visible in the lower right corner. This area of Canadian is still a vital business area and the site of renewal as the 20th century closes.

The Killarney Café (shown above) was founded before 1933 at Second and Main Streets, and was purchased in 1937 by Naceeb Abraham. Naceeb's younger brother, Malouf "Oofie," helped manage the business while Naceeb served in World War II. This was a popular eating place for many years in Canadian.

In 1938, Nahim Abraham bought the former girls' dormitory (shown above) from the Whitsels. The family undertook a renovation to provide the Mediterranean look of their native Lebanon. In 1938, traveling by ocean liner to visit Lebanon, they purchased many items including a Persian rug. Nahim's admonition to his descendants was "To whom much is given, much is expected," a reference to the freedom and to the economic opportunities offered by America.

Alice Moody Tubb (seated, center) is shown above with her eight surviving children. From left to right are (women) Dora, Juanita, Ruth, Mae, and Sue; (men) Charlie, Earl, and George. One child died in infancy in England before the family came to America, and a second child died in 1893 in Hemphill County.

The Hobdy Motor Company was started by R. M. Hobdy, who came to Canadian in 1916. He worked as a mechanic for the Tubb Motor Company, a Ford dealership in the early 1920s. A Chrysler-Plymouth dealership was operated at Third and Main Streets until 1933, at which time Maurice Hobdy took on a Ford dealership. On May 1, 1948, the Ford dealership was moved to the building on Highway 60/83 shown above. (Courtesy of Buddy Hobdy.)

Joseph "Joe" Reid Sr. came to Hemphill County with his parents and siblings in 1908, where they farmed in the Zybach community. He later owned the dealership, Reid Chevrolet, on Main Street. The dealership moved to Highway 60 (shown above) and was managed by J. B. Reid Jr. until it was sold in 1971, and he entered the insurance business.

Shown above is the building at 118 North Third Street, the final home for the *Hemphill County News* from 1938 to 1968. The building, which had been a post office and a grocery store, was purchased by the Miller family from Lena Tipps in 1947. The newspaper ceased publication at the death of its editor/publisher Othello Miller in 1968. Elna Miller used the building as the Gift Area until 1993. (Courtesy of Colette Miller Valles.)

Earl Blackmore early cattle trucks are proudly lined up for viewing. Blackmore would deliver cattle to the railhead from the various ranches. Pictured above are three Fords, one Chevrolet, and one GMC.

14 tons Broom Corn raised by one man on 60 acres, sold for $160.00 per ton. Canadian, Tex.

Broom corn is not really a corn at all. It is more of a tall grass that forms a majestic fan-shaped seed head instead of ears of corn. Broom corn is truly used to make brooms, and it is difficult for one man to raise and harvest the 14 tons noted in the above picture, particularly in the early 1900s.

In 1904, W. R. Hext (shown above, far left) purchased a section of the old Laurel Leaf Ranch and moved his family to Hemphill County. The other men in the picture are R. B. Wiggins, J. L. Jennings, and Tom Connell. W. R. Hext was a widower with nine children in 1893 when he met and married Dora Birmingham, who was a widow with three children. Together they had a total of 19 children by the time of his death in 1930. The ranching tradition continues in this family today. Shown at right are four of the Hext children: (first row) Relia (left) and Lila; (second row) Bob (left) and Hub. Hub went on to be a much-loved teacher in the Canadian schools.

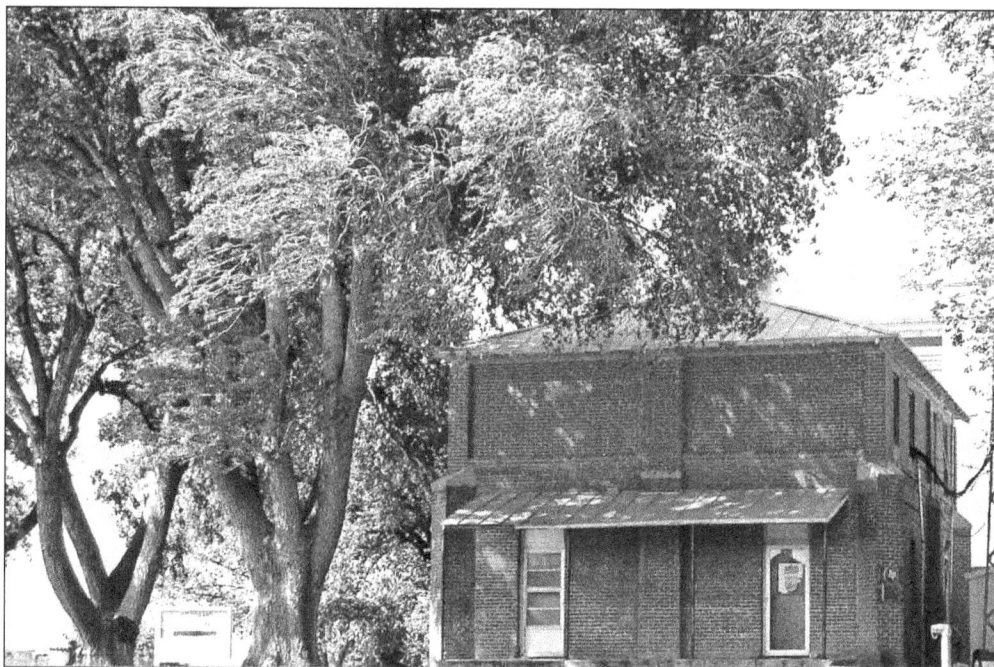

The first jail was a wooden building replaced in 1890 by a two-story brick jail, shown above. This jail held notorious bank robber Pete Traxler, who was wanted in several Oklahoma and Texas counties for bank and highway robbery, and the murder of a deputy sheriff in Oklahoma in the mid-1930s. On May 10, 1936, he was caught at a roadblock on the Canadian River Bridge manned by about 10 officers, including Lipscomb County deputy Elmer Tarbox, shown below at left, and Hemphill County deputy Harry Rathjen, shown below at right. The *Amarillo Daily News* reported, upon Sheriff Tarbox's retirement, that "while serving nearly 30 years in public office in a rather remote ranching area, he had more exciting experiences than many globetrotters." (Both, courtesy of Gayle Haygood.)

Six

WAR AND RECOVERY
1940–1969

The 1910 Canadian High School, located at Fifth Street and Kingman Avenue, was replaced in 1939–1940 when the new building was constructed with the assistance of the Works Progress Administration (WPA) at 404 Sixth Street. This photograph shows Canadian High School as it appeared in 1945.

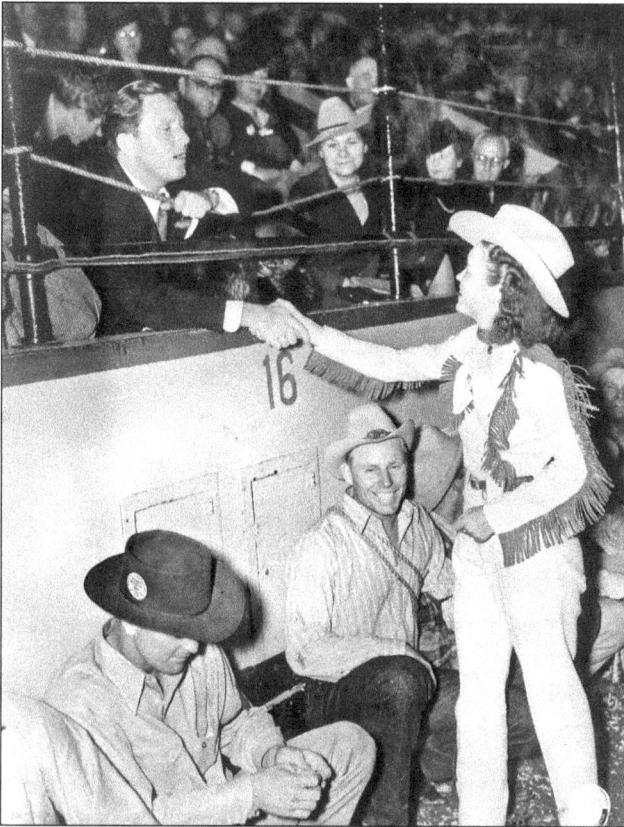

Sydna Yokley (shown below on School Boy) was raised on the Yokley ranch outside Canadian, Texas. She developed riding and roping skills as a young girl, and in the 1940s and 1950s, she was noted for her achievements as a top-flight calf roper. Yokley's 28-day performance in Madison Square Garden and two-week performance at Boston Gardens in 1939 prompted a *Life* magazine article. While at Madison Square Garden in 1939, Sydna met Spencer Tracey (at left), who was in the audience. Sydna Yokley Woodyard was tragically killed on July 25, 1959, while traveling from California to Canadian. She stopped at Winslow, Arizona, to check on her horse, and the horse panicked, tossed his head, knocking Sydna unconscious, and trampled her to death in the horse trailer.

Hemphill County had its share of nationally ranked rodeo cowboys. The Hill brothers started their rodeo careers at Anvil Park Rodeo on the J. C. Studer Ranch in 1938. Clinton, shown above, joined the Professional Turtle Rodeo Association ("slow to organize") in 1941 at Texarkana, Texas, and was the youngest rodeo contestant at that time. Clayton, shown below, joined the Professional Rodeo Cowboys Association (PRCA) in 1944 in Cheyenne, Wyoming. Clinton said that it was an honor in 1953 when he led several months for the title of World's Champion Saddle Bronc Rider. Clayton, at one point, was also in the lead for the World's Champion Bull Rider title until he broke his leg that same year. Clinton and Clayton participated for more than 25 years in rodeo. Both received a Gold Card from the PRCA.

Bill George (leaning toward the calf) was one of the cowboys who competed during the "Golden Age of Rodeo" in the 1950s. He competed in the timed events, such as the steer wrestling (shown above), and in the rough stock events, such as bareback broncs and bull riding. His main claim to fame was when he and his wife, Billie Lewis George, manufactured cowboy hats under the name of "American Hats, the cowboy's favorite."

Shown at left is Charlie Tubb standing next to his car in the early 1940s among his cattle on Elk Creek Ranch. Tubb came to Hemphill County at the age of 10 with his mother and father, George Charles Louis Tubb and Alice Moody Tubb, in 1887 and settled on this ranch. They lived in a two-room dugout until they built their two-story home on the ranch. (Courtesy of Gena Tubb.)

Shown above is an accidental double exposure—one picture of a moving tractor and one of Dorsey Tubb, son of Charles Tubb, drinking water out of the old-fashioned double-sided water can lid. Dorsey welded and attached the sun shade on the tractor. Dorsey was one of the first farmers in Hemphill County to use methods to conserve moisture and keep stubble on top of the ground to combat erosion. (Courtesy of Gena Tubb.)

In 1948, the Caylor hospital was replaced by the new Hemphill County Hospital, located at 905 Cheyenne Avenue (shown above). Hemphill County has been fortunate to have excellent care from many good physicians, including Drs. E. H. and Rush Snyder, E. H. Morris, A. N. Newman, F. D. Teas, Teddy Darocha, Malouf Abraham Jr., William Isaacs, and Valerie Verbi.

Shown to the left, in 1951, the wagon bridge used for automobile traffic across the Canadian River was severely damaged by flood conditions. A new bridge was built to completely replace the old wagon bridge. Both Sanford Dam in Texas and the Conchas Reservoir in New Mexico were constructed, in part, to provide water for the Canadian River Basin and to control flooding.

While the bridge was out, students from north of the river needed a means to get to school in Canadian. The Santa Fe Railroad instituted passenger service, the shortest route in its history, from the north side of the Canadian River to the depot and back each day. Shown above are the schoolchildren with J. W. Sutton, the Baker Elementary principal. (Courtesy of Judy Wooten.)

The Gilman Flowers family moved to Hemphill County in 1946 and built the ranch house shown above. From left to right, Vickie, Pat, and Zella Flowers, three of their nine children, are shown in the photograph. The generosity of Lois and Gilman Flowers ensured that all the children still have farming and ranching interests today. The Flowers family have always been strong supporters of the First Baptist Church, and Gilman Flowers served on the Canadian Independent School District School Board for many years. (Courtesy of Frances Flowers Newell.)

Reid Errington (pictured at right) opened his saddle shop in Canadian in 1947. A talented artist, Reid combined hand-stamped original floral patterns with the best of materials and workmanship to make saddles capable of withstanding the roughest range use. His saddles can be found in every state in the Union. He made saddles for singer Allan Jones and cowboy star Leo Carrillo, "Pancho," the sidekick of the "Cisco Kid." (Courtesy of Gayle Haygood.)

The "old" Baker School (shown above) was built at Cheyenne Avenue and Sixth Street, and was named for the town's first attorney and early judge, B. M. Baker. A "new" Baker School was built in 1955. The Baker Schools housed grades 1 through 6, with the grades 4 through 6 classrooms in the "old" Baker. Consequently, the Mary Brainard Isaacs School on Main and Ninth Streets, which had been built in 1907, closed its doors in September 1955. Shown below is Lillian Carr's fourth-grade class from 1957 in front of the "old" Baker School. (Below, courtesy of Sue Lynn Krehbiel.)

Canadian's first city-owned swimming pool was built behind the city hall on First Street and opened on Memorial Day 1955. A summer-long swimming ticket cost $7, and instruction in swimming and Water Safety Instruction (WSI) for future lifeguards were provided in the mornings.

The First State Bank was chartered in 1953 with directors G. B. Mathers, Frank McMordie, R. T. "Cap" Kelley, J. M. Crews, Charles Wright, Arthur "Bud" Webb, Joe Reid, and Frank J. Shaller, along with John D. Glenn as executive vice president. It opened in the old First National Bank building at Third and Main Streets, and moved to Second and Main Streets (shown above) in 1970. It continues to operate today.

Needing more space, ground-breaking for the present First Baptist Church (shown above) at Main and Seventh Streets was held in 1953. By 1954, the Fellowship Hall, basement, and education wing were dedicated. Further construction occurred in 1959 of a bell tower, offices, and a sanctuary. More additions were made in 1980.

In April 1951, for the second time in its history, the Santa Fe Roundhouse was destroyed by fire, as shown above. This fire was caused by the explosion of a locomotive boiler, and Bill McPherson, a railway mechanic, lost his life. The roundhouse was not rebuilt by Santa Fe, and in 1954, Santa Fe moved its freight terminal to Amarillo, 110 miles away.

For more than 50 years, an annual carnival sponsored by school classes and organizations was held in the city hall at Halloween. Shown above are some of the booths that completely filled the auditorium, giving those sponsors an opportunity to raise funds for school events. During the carnival, townspeople would vote for a Carnival Queen and her court, one princess from each of the four high school classes. Shown below are the 1958 Carnival Queen, Jackie Sharp, and her escort, Harold Yarnold.

The Nahim Abraham family founded the Edward Abraham Memorial Home to honor their son, who passed away in 1961. The home, shown above, opened in 1964 and was one of the first nursing homes in this area of the Panhandle. It continues today as a nonprofit organization.

Shown above are George and Polly Tubb behind their sons, David (left) and Gary, in a 1963 photograph taken at Camp Perry, Ohio. All four members of this family regularly competed at the NRA (National Rifle Association) Rifle Championships. Polly and George began as competitive shooters and winners in the 1950s. By the 1970s, both sons were competing as well. David has more National High Power Match Rifle Championships than any other competitor.

Shown to the right is Maudaline Hutton, a fixture in the Canadian Public Schools as a principal, master teacher, advisor, librarian, and friend. Her impact on two generations of students and the community at large was honored when the 1960 issue of the school's yearbook, *The Beargrass*, was dedicated to her. She retired in 1970 after 44 years of teaching and school administration in Canadian.

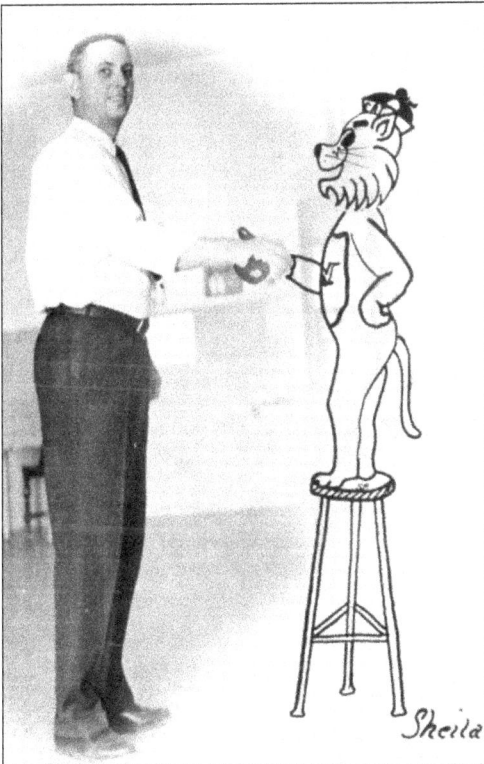

Joe Cullender (shown above) came to Canadian as the high school principal in 1960 and later served the district as superintendent. He nurtured the school system through a period of growth and change with a steady and firm hand. He earned respect for his administrative and people skills, whether responding to pigs hidden in the gym over a weekend or working with the school board on expansion projects.

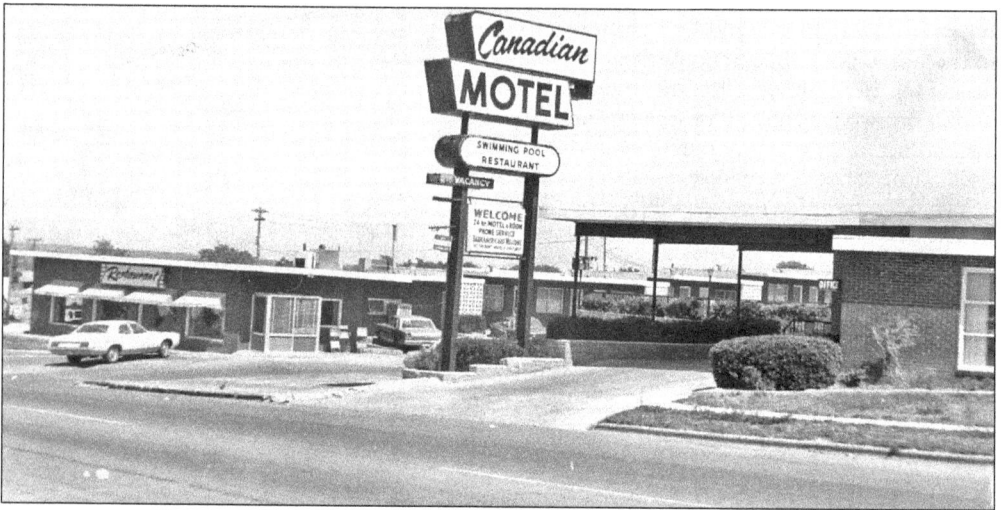

Shown above, the Canadian Motel and Restaurant (at left) was built by Malouf Abraham in the 1950s and served the community for many years. A former Harvey Girl, Alice Garnas, was an especially efficient and friendly fixture in the restaurant. The Canadian Restaurant continues to operate today, although now at 402 North Second Street.

After the heavy damage to the wagon bridge in 1951, construction began on the new bridge shown above, which opened for service in 1953 and remains in use today as part of Highway 60/83.

The Canadian Abundant Life Assembly of God was established in 1936 with charter members Dora Hazelwood, Mrs. Bert Porter, and Mrs. S. A. Bentley. A church was constructed at Third Street and Kingman Avenue in 1945 when Dora Hazelwood contributed money received from the government upon the death of her soldier son. In 1976, the church constructed a new building, shown above, on Birch Street.

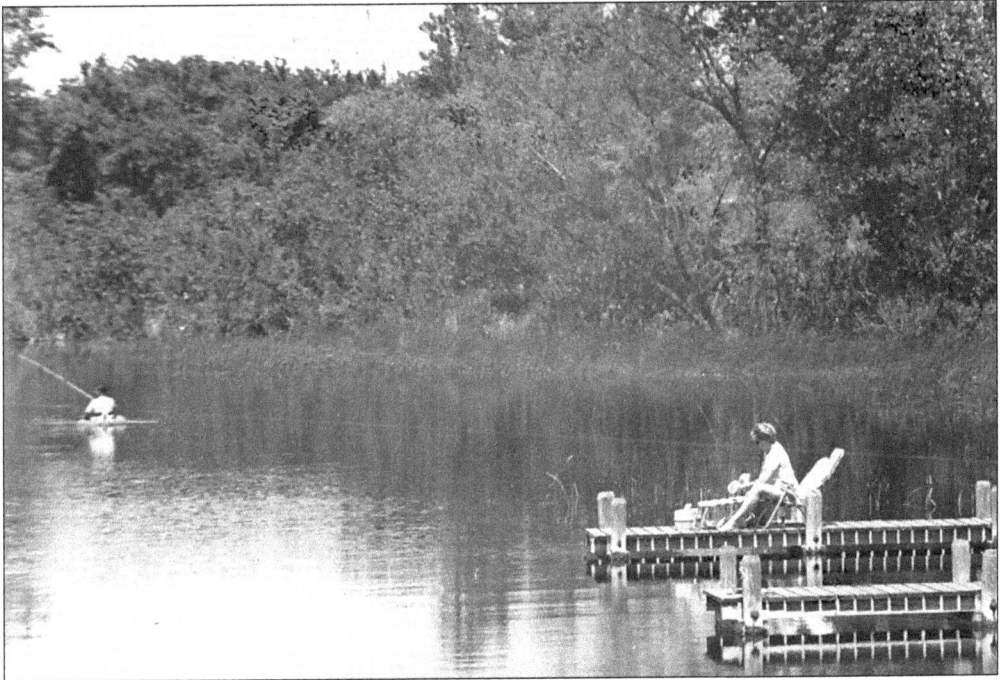

Lake Marvin is an artificial lake constructed in the 1930s on Boggy Creek in east central Hemphill County by the Panhandle Water Conservation Authority. Its purpose is primarily for soil conservation, flood control, recreation, and promotion of wildlife. The reservoir was named in honor of Marvin Jones, a retired judge of the U.S. Supreme Court of Claims. The Black Kettle National Grassland surrounds it.

The seeds of the University Interscholastic League (UIL) were planted in 1904 in a decision that the University of Texas needed to serve to the entire state. Canadian schools joined in 1917, and by 1955, a tradition of annual state winners began in the numerous categories. Shown above is the Slide Rule club of 1964, including special mention of Wade Adams as a first-place winner.

In 1965, mascot Willie the Wildcat, drawn by Shelia Foster, made his first appearance in the school and *The Beargrass* annual for that year. Willie began as a drawing by student Sheila Foster, and by 1973, he was a fixture at various sports events. "He" is often portrayed by a girl and is elected by the student body.

90

Seven

WAVES THE BLACK AND GOLD
1970–1989

The impact of oil production on Hemphill County is extensive. In the 1970s, the first real boom began. King Rig No. 10 is shown above in a "swabbing" operation in the mid-1980s. When a well is loaded with fluid and is not strong enough to unload itself, "swabbing" allows the fluid to be pulled out by pulling the rods until the well becomes strong enough to perform the operation on its own. (Courtesy of King Well Service, Inc.)

Shown above is an aerial photograph of the Hemphill County Fair during the opening of the Hemphill County Exhibition Center in the mid-1980s. The original King Rig No. 1 is pictured directly outside of exhibition, and the original King Rig No. 9 is shown in the top right corner of photograph. (Courtesy of King Well Service, Inc.)

In 1976, a new Hemphill County Hospital was constructed at 1020 South Fourth Street. The hospital eventually would accommodate a physicians' clinic and imaging capabilities, both key items for attracting medical professionals to the basically rural community.

The Church of Christ, founded in 1903, constructed its first building in 1910. In 1921, the congregation created the Canadian Orphan's Home when a church member died, leaving four small children. The unused Baptist Academy was a temporary location for the orphan's home, which moved to Tipton, Oklahoma, in 1924. In 1975, a new building (shown above) was constructed at South Fourth and Cedar Streets.

In 1971, Rachel's Little House (pictured above) was founded by the Presbyterian Women's Association under the direction of Rachel Snyder, wife to Dr. Rush Snyder Jr. Rachel's Little House remains the primary source for preschool care and instruction today with funding from several local organizations. In December 1981, the First Presbyterian Church assumed responsibility for Rachel's Little House for the Snyders and for the community.

In 1976, a new Canadian High School (shown above) was built on the former athletic field, and the 1939–1940 vintage high school building became the Canadian Middle School. Hemphill County was in the midst of an oil boom, and the Independent School District administration and trustees used the funds well to provide for the consequent growth in students. Wildcat Stadium, shown below, was built at Cedar and Locust Streets on a site that formed a natural bowl, and the winning football tradition continued. This new Wildcat Stadium offers one of the best views of any high school venue in the state.

Albert Paul Liske was a German immigrant to the Texas Panhandle who, after settling in Canadian, founded the Liske Grain Company. In April 1930, the Liske Grain Company offered a trophy to the best all-around Canadian High School student. Many recipients have proceeded to be exceptional citizens in communities across the nation. Shown at right is Mike Schafer, winner of the 1977 Liske Cup.

Mike Schafer
Liske Cup

The Liske Cup is the highest award given to any graduating student of Canadian High School. A committee consisting of the Superintendent, the Senior Sponsor, the Principal, a Coach and a member of the faculty meet and score each Senior according to his or her participation in School Activities and various other requirements. The scoring consists of the following: Scholarship 30 pts., Leadership 10 pts., Citizenship and School Attitude 20 pts., Sportsmanship 10 pts., Various School Activities 10 pts.

Liske Cup winners are expected to excel in all the above areas and are to be well liked and respected among their fellow students as well as members of the administration. They must also be grade-wise, in the top five of the Senior class. Mike met and excelled in all of these requirements and we know he will have a very promising future.

The Abraham Award is given to the most outstanding student in the Eighth Grade being promoted into Canadian High School. The winner of the award is unknown until the night of Middle School Graduation. The winner is selected by the same committee which selects the Liske Cup Winner. The winner is selected on much the same basis as that of the Liske Cup Winner. The winner must have been enrolled in Canadian Middle School all three years. A grade average of Eighty is required and the higher the grade average a student has, the more points he or she earns. He or she must have participated in school activities such as Band, UIL events, and Boys or Girls' Athletics. They must have an outgoing school spirit and pride and be friendly to fellow students and faculty members. The Award was set up by the Abraham family in memory of Edward Abraham. Any student receiving both the Abraham Award and the Liske Cup is given a gift of two hundred by Malouf Abraham Sr.

Mike Mitchell
Abraham Award

The Abraham Award is given to the eighth-grade student with the best all-around performance. Its prestige matches that associated with the Liske Cup. The award was founded by Malouf Abraham Sr. in 1951. Until his death in 1994, students who earned both awards were given $200 from Malouf Abraham upon graduation from Canadian High School. Current graduates receive $500. Shown at left is Mike Mitchell, who won the award in 1977.

In October 1981, a plan to purchase the 1948 Hemphill County Hospital building, then vacant, was initiated. Plans to use the building as a YMCA (Young Men's Christian Association) were jump-started when the Iris and Malouf Abraham Foundation contributed $100,000. Matching funds were raised by the community, and this important asset was born.

First Row: Paula Swindle, Becky Bennett, Mary Pickens, Stephany Scroggins, Doris Doughty, Janie Taylor. Second Row: Sherry Davis, Lori Campbell, Laquita Stark, Peggy Carter, Cindy Adcock, Annette Rex. Third Row: Mrs. Ullom, Sally Mathews, Cindy Waterfield, Donna Bruce, Vicki Thomson, Kathy Sansing, Deanna McCook, Katrina Walser, Mrs. Stanton. Fourth Row: Paula McCook, Gwen Walser, Dena Moore, Kim Morrow.

The FHA organization is an important part of the homemaking education program. It provides additional experiences in planning and carrying out activities related to home, school, and community.

Another part of the Home Ec. department is H.E.C.E. This program prepares students for employment in occupations requiring knowledge and skills in one or more of the following Home Ec. areas: child development, clothing textiles, consumer education, family living, and housing.

Officers

President	Katrina Walser
Vice President	Jan Owens
Secretary	Sally Mathews
Treasurer	Gwen Walser
Reporter	Tracy Wilson
Song Leader	Becky Bennett
Parliamentarian	Mary Pickens

The Future Homemakers of America (FHA) began on June 11, 1945. It was created in Chicago, Illinois, by Edna P. Amidon. The name of the organization was changed to Family, Career, and Community Leaders of America (FCCLA) in July 1999. Shown at left is the 1977 organization at Canadian High School.

By 1973, Willie the Wildcat had become a "human" representation of the drawn mascot made famous in 1965. Attending all football and basketball games and pep rallies, Willie had become an integral part of the enthusiasm accompanying these events. Shown at right is Tammy Benge, Willie for 1973.

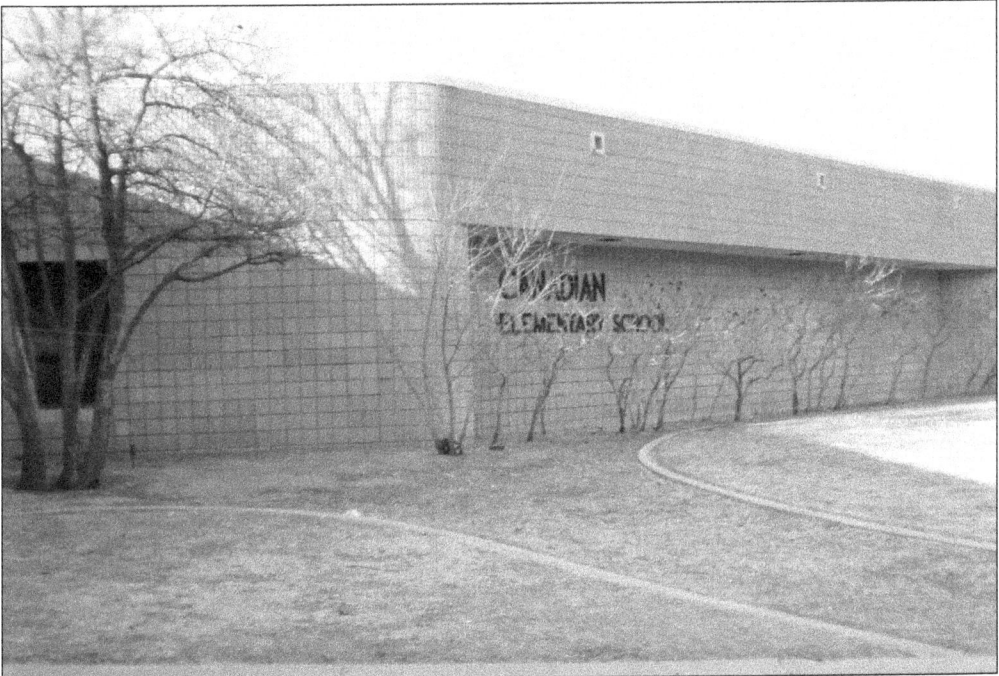

Increased growth resulted in the construction of a modern elementary school in 1984 at 500 Dogwood Street, shown above. First through third grades benefited from the school, which included a cafeteria, meaning students no longer had to leave the building to attend lunch.

A charming old wooden house was on this corner and was owned by the Sheets family. The house was partially burned and the trees and sidewalks were damaged, so the Abraham Trust bought the corner, and Dr. Malouf Abraham designed a gazebo, shown at left. The corner was given to the First Presbyterian Church for use by the community. This corner was turned from a wreck to a beauty spot on this busy street.

The Canadian Volunteer Fire Department, originally located at the city hall, moved across Main Street to the new fire station, shown above, in the early 1970s. Through the years, this volunteer organization has been effective in responding to fires in Hemphill and surrounding counties.

Hemphill County's Volunteer Fire Department is shown above in one of two photographs taken in the early 1970s. Pictured from left to right are (first row) Lester Hodges, Frankie Carver, Gene Mathews, Bill Hodges, and R. T. Smith; (second row) Frank Guthrie, Jerry McElreath, Joe Schaef, and Tom Goodwin. With some duplication, the remaining firefighters are shown below, from left to right, (first row) Joe Schaef, Bill Britton, Buddy Hobdy, Sandy Fiel, John Whitsett, and Bill Hodges; (second row) Gerhardt Koch, Frankie Carver, R. L. Anderson, R. T. Smith, Lawrence Teague, and Frank Guthrie.

Carrie's Corner, shown above, opened in October 1978 in the Main Street space that was formerly Dr. E. H. Morris's office. In 2000, owner Sue Cecotti moved the renamed Canadian Florist to the 200 block of Main Street, where it remains today. (Courtesy of Sue Cecotti.)

On March 2, 1981, the Zybach-Owens American Legion building, leased to the Canadian Mill Works, burned, as shown in the above photograph. The building was used for grading and sorting lumber. The large amount of burning cardboard caused the black smoke. Fortunately, the fire occurred 30 minutes after the day's work had ended, and there were no injuries.

Neal and Vivian Beasley came to Canadian in 1948, and in 1963, Vivian opened her first donut shop, operating it for seven years. Neal put in Ma Beasley's Donut Shop in March 1984, knowing he had terminal cancer and that Vivian could support herself with a job she loved. Ma Beasley's is operated today at 316 Main Street by Alice and Daniel Ferguson.

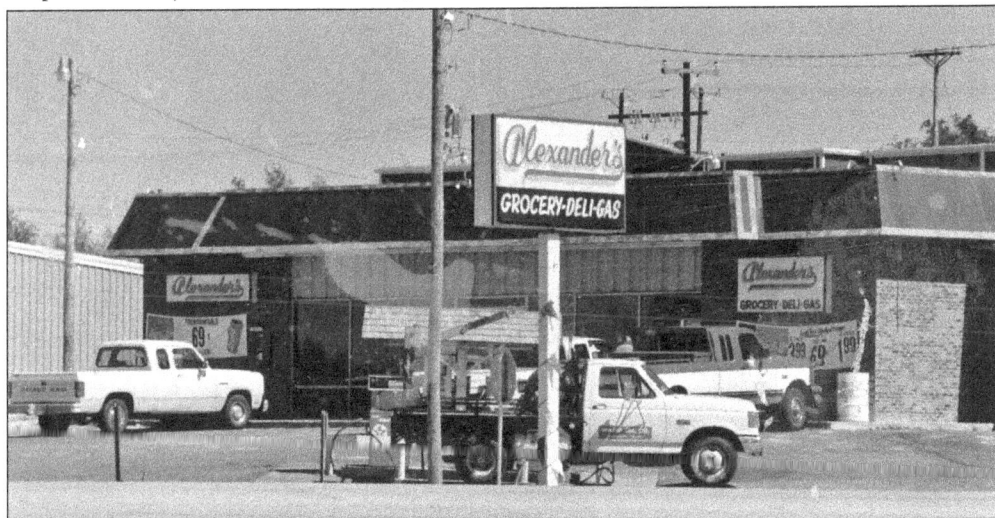

Alexander's Grocery and Deli at Highway 60 and Birch Street (shown above) was founded in 1988 by Tim Alexander and quickly became a popular noontime gathering and eating place for the town of Canadian. A monthly "menu" of meals of the day is posted in the *Canadian Record*, and Alexander even takes the homemade food on the road as a caterer to oil sites and organizations throughout town. (Courtesy of Tim Alexander.)

In May 1986, three tornado funnel clouds approached Hemphill County, as shown above. Shortly thereafter (below), a larger tornado, accompanied by marble- and baseball-sized hail, "touched" the ground, destroying electric high lines about 7 miles west of Canadian. Fortunately, ample warning was received, so there were no injuries. Tornado watches and warnings are a regular occurrence in Hemphill County, as they are throughout the Great Plains. (Both, courtesy of Frances Flowers Newell.)

The Comancheria (ko-man'-chi-ria, land of the Comanches) Chapter of the Daughters of the American Revolution (DAR) was organized on April 14, 1973, in Canadian, Texas, by Al'Louise Suthers Ramp. DAR chapters promote patriotism, historic preservation, and education, and this chapter is active in all three objectives. Shown above, from left to right, are the charter members: (first row) Mabel Forgey, Lisbeth Mitchell, Al'Louise Ramp, Blanche Hyde, Wyonne McDaniel, Janet Parnell, and Mary Ann Ashley; (second row) Norene Morse, Virginia Whipple, Nancy McIntyre, Toni Watson, Nancy Coffee, Eleanor Worsham, Ellen Huff, Cornelia Varnell, Cindy Wheeler, Libby Barker, and Davene Hendershot. Below is a Fourth of July parade float (Sweepstakes Award Winner) honoring early pioneer women of Canadian: civic leader (Al'Louise Ramp); saloon girl (Deana Gardiner); nurse (Cornelia Varnell); rodeo queen (Marilee Wright); ranch wife (Gena Tubb); and teacher (Mary Ann Ashley). (Above, courtesy of Mary Ann Ashley; below, courtesy of Gena Tubb.)

In 1978, a group of Hemphill County women met at the home of Polly Tubb to organize the Sagebrush Painters. This group has contributed significantly to the interest of art in Canadian, hosting workshops and exhibiting at an annual Fourth of July Art Show. Shown above, from left to right, are some of the participants: Math Keim, Kathryn Jones, Polly Tubb, Mary Williams, Bea Moon, Ehtel Adcock, Shirlene Vines, Fern Young, Lana Rogers Gardner, and Gwen Suthers. (Courtesy of Polly Tubb.)

D. F. Urschel came to Hemphill County in 1923 and purchased the land currently known as the Urschel Ranch. His grandson, Dan, and his wife, Jolene, purchased Special Effort, shown above, in 1981. The winner of 13 of 14 races, Special Effort retired with earnings of $1,219,949 and was the first ever to win the American Quarter Horse Association's Triple Crown for two-year-olds. Through his progeny, he has had a lasting effect on the breed. (Courtesy of Dan Urschel.)

Eight

BOOM AGAIN
1990–2000

Denny McLanahan from Canadian rose to the top, staying there longer and earning more than anyone else from Hemphill County. Beginning in high school, through college, and as a professional, McLanahan eventually specialized in bareback riding, as shown above in the 1998 National Finals Rodeo in Las Vegas, a year he was voted fan favorite in a contest to recognize cowboys who have made a positive impact on rodeo fans.

A fourth generation of the Nahim Abraham family continues to prosper in Hemphill County. Sons of Dr. Malouf and Therese Abraham Jr., grandsons of Malouf Sr., Eddie (left) is a ranch manager of a successful cow/calf operation and his brother, Salem (center) is founder and president of Abraham Trading Company, located on the second floor of the Moody Hotel. This firm, on some days, represents one percent of the trading volume on the Chicago Mercantile Exchanges. Brother Jason (right) initiated a program of leasing healthy mares for embryo transplants. The brothers co-own the Abraham Land and Cattle Company in the Mendota area of Hemphill County and have continued the Abraham tradition of philanthropy and civic involvement. Shown below is a Salem Abraham project, the renovated Palace Theater, one of only four in Texas with a high-fidelity THX digital sound system. (Above, courtesy of Dr. Malouf Abraham; below, courtesy of Barnett Photography.)

Rose Marie Miller Bentley founded the monthly *Hemphill County Free Press* in 1997. Rose grew up in her parents' *Hemphill County News* office and developed a love for writing. The free paper, supported by local advertising, contained human interest and history stories, and recipes, poems, and jokes submitted by readers. Her motto for the paper was "It will always be clean and never be mean." (Courtesy of Colette Miller Valles.)

Every five years, all past Canadian High School graduates and their families are invited to return for an All School Reunion. Special recognition is awarded to the class with the highest percentage of attending graduates and to the oldest attending graduate. The photograph above shows only one-third of a full gymnasium at the 1995 All School Reunion. Each class separates later into parties held all over the county. (Courtesy of the *Canadian Record*.)

The River Valley Pioneer Museum houses more than 7,000 artifacts provided by an estimated 380 donors. More than 3,000 people visit the museum annually, which has also preserved and digitized approximately 5,000 glass and soft negatives from early photographer Julius Born. The museum, through generous donations and grants, plays host to the annual Fourth of July Old Timer's Reunion and Fall Foliage Quilt Show and numerous other events.

Shown above, the Hemphill County Veterans Memorial was dedicated on November 11, 1991. All veterans, both in peacetime and wartime, are listed on the memorial. A special section is given to those who lost their life in service to the country. The monument committee was composed of Marie Killebrew, Bill Hodges, Rodney Bass, and Lee Chumbly.

Shown above is the modern wagon bridge as it appears in 2000, now a walking trail across the Canadian River. Many citizens assisted in funding to preserve and restore this bridge. Its presence as a walking bridge connects many with the ecosystem of the Canadian River. Shown below is a view that does not exaggerate the length of the bridge. The splendid views along the mile-long walk are a special attraction for both local enthusiasts and visitors.

Laura's Flowers is located at 212 North Seventh Street across from the Caylor hospital, which is now a residence. Laura Wilson purchased Hill's Florist in 1975 at this site and encouraged customers to "come by and put a little color in your world."

The Future Farmers of America (FFA) was founded nationally in 1928 to bring students, educators, and agribusiness together. The name was changed to the National FFA Organization in 1988, and Canadian High School's chapter regularly places well in FFA leadership and career development events. Strong financial support at stock shows is received from local agribusiness organizations, farmers, and ranchers. Shown above is the 1996 FFA organization of young men and women.

Shown above is an aerial view of Canadian taken in the 1990s. Highway 60 (Second Street) intersects Main Street. Shown in the lower right-hand corner is the River Valley Pioneer Museum next to the First State Bank, which is across Main Street from the Moody Hotel. Proceeding three blocks to the left on Main Street is a portion of the Hemphill County Courthouse shown on the extreme left.

This aerial view shows the sports complex to the north of town just off Highway 60. Osborne Park is named for county commissioner Kenneth Osborne, who strongly advocated the creation of the new site for Little League baseball. Previously, Rotary Park could only accommodate one game at a time, and this complex increased that to four.

Hemphill County is far enough north to experience fall color, a novelty for much of the Panhandle. The Annual Foliage Tour in Hemphill County attracts thousands to events, including the River Valley Pioneer Museum Quilt Show, as seen above, tours of local homes, and drives through the Gene Howe Wildlife Refuge and around Lake Marvin.

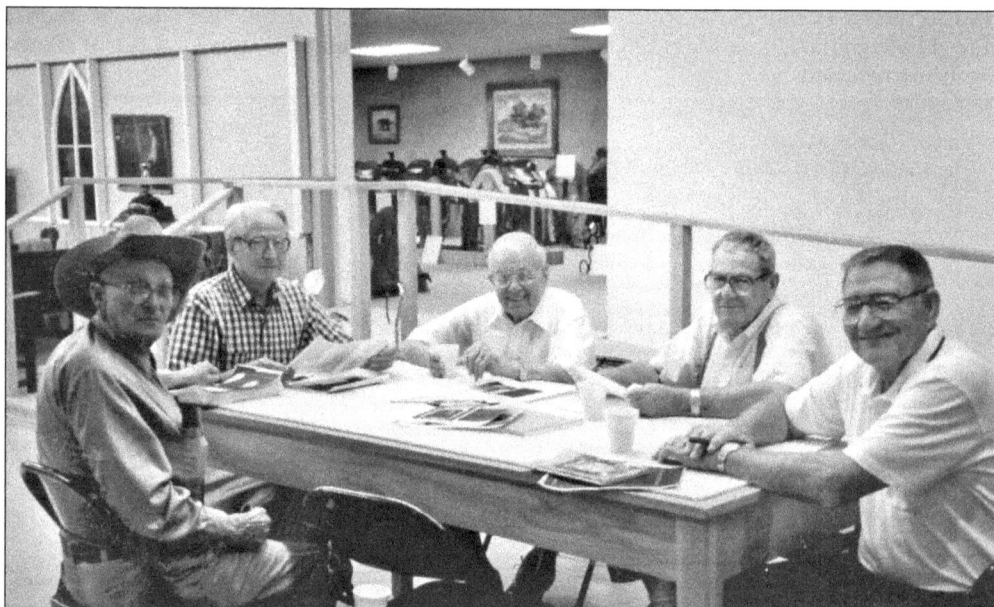

Julius Born, early photographer and sarsaparilla maker in Hemphill County, left approximately 5,000 glass and soft negatives, which have been digitized and are available for viewing at the River Valley Pioneer Museum. A group of local "experts," shown above, reviewed the negatives, attempting to associate names with the 95 percent Julius Born had failed to identify. Those sitting are, from left to right, Horace River, Erbin Crowell, Tom Abraham, Buddy Hobdy, and Don Schaef.

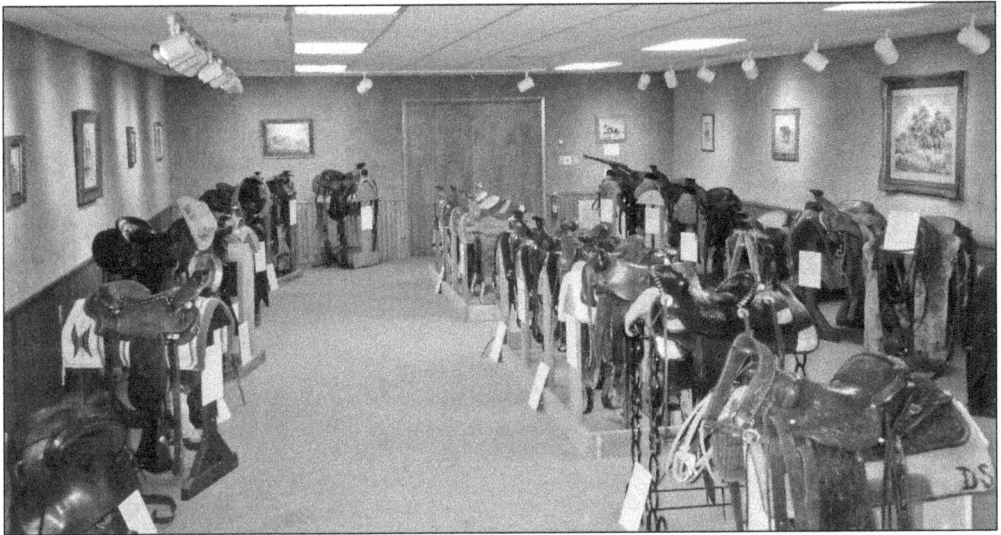

Shown in the photograph above is one of the many temporary exhibits that grace the gallery funded by the Malouf and Iris Abraham 1982 Charitable Lead Trust at the River Valley Pioneer Museum. Although some exhibits travel among community museums, this one represented Hemphill County–owned saddles of all ages. Those won in rodeo competition were displayed next to saddles used on the range 100 years ago.

Canadian High School saw the creation of a Students Against Drunk Driving (SADD) chapter in 1997 after the untimely death of Kami Michelle Minick two days before the start of her senior year. The organization, which stresses a drug- and alcohol-free lifestyle, remains one of the larger student organizations at Canadian High School, as the photograph above from the 2000 *Beargrass* shows.

The 2000 Canadian High School Student Council, shown above, is composed of class representatives. They sponsor many functions throughout the year, including painting the gold Wildcat paw prints on the streets from the highway, leading soon-to-be-defeated opponents to the stadium.

A new century for Hemphill County and Canadian High School is ushered in by the cheerleaders and Willie the Wildcat, shown in this 2000 photograph from *The Beargrass*. Those pictured, from left to right, are Jennifer Hale, Kim Long, Kathy Lee, Darcey Wyche (Willie), Kris Ward, Betsy Hill, and Jokari Davis.

Nine

COMMUNITIES
GONE BUT NOT FORGOTTEN

Mendota, on Red Deer Creek in western Hemphill County, was established in 1887 and moved in 1907 to its final site on the Panhandle and Santa Fe Railroad route. The Union Church and school cornerstones were laid in 1909. Most of the populace did their trading at nearby Canadian, and the town remained, serving as a stock-loading center for area ranchers and farmers. The post office was discontinued in the early 1940s and the school in 1945. (Courtesy of Rhea Wilson.)

The photograph at the left is of the Mendota school class of 1928. Families represented in the picture include the Ortegas, Killebrews, Wilsons, and Chaffins. Schoolteachers for the school, which was closed in 1945, included Harley Wright, Leola Fillingem, Madeline Crosier, and Alice Meadows. (Courtesy of Rhea Wilson.)

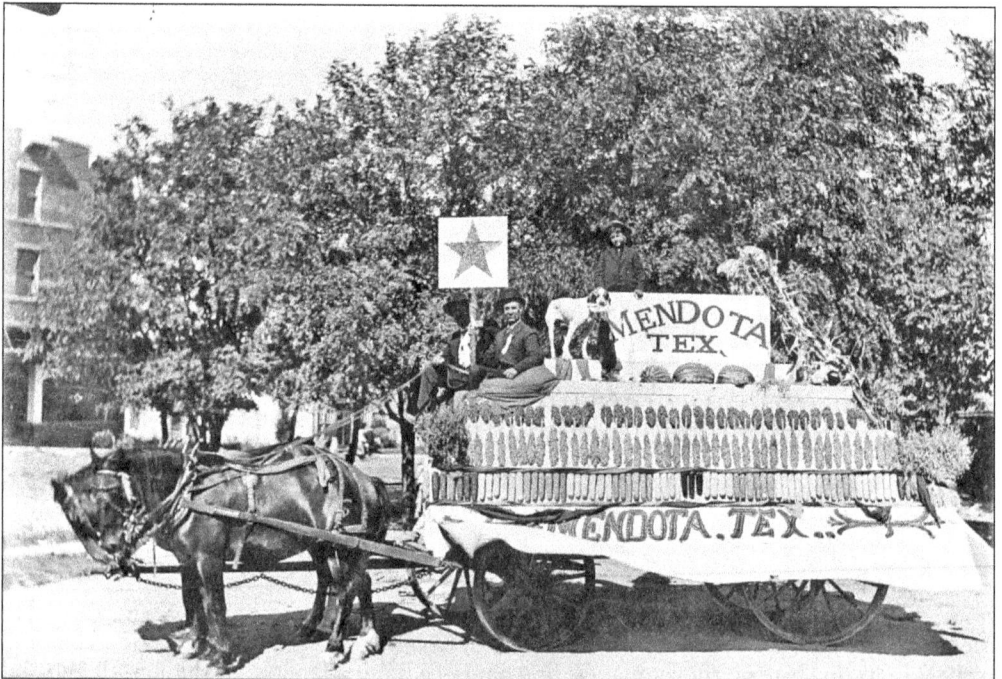

Mendota's float in the 1910 Texas-Oklahoma Fair parade is shown in this photograph. The dog and the two gentlemen in the seat are unidentified. Although the community thrived until the 1940s, it is a ghost town today.

Gageby, in southern Hemphill County, was named for the nearby creek. The town was founded in 1907, and a post office opened at the home/store of A. A. Hennington in 1910, as seen in the above photograph. The population ranged from 10 to 50, and the post office closed in 1954.

Shown above is Gem City, named for Gem Hibbard Moody, which existed on the eastern side of Hemphill County. The Moody Land Company began selling lots at an auction on July 4, 1909. A blacksmith shop owned by F. W. Coyn, a branch of the Tepe-Hoover Lumber Company, and a Buckner-McAdams store provided easy access to the products of the day.

The Gem and Prairie Dell community schools consolidated with the Blue Ridge School, shown above, in the late 1940s. The Blue Ridge School had been founded in 1907 and was moved at least twice. Students at Blue Ridge rode a bus into Canadian once they were in the seventh grade and were noted for the high quality of education they had received to that point. In 1970, Blue Ridge was the last community school to be annexed by the Canadian Independent School District. Shown below is one of the Blue Ridge School's girls' group photographs from the late 1950s. From left to right are (first row) Jane Forrest, Sydna Moore, Ruth Forrest, Janis Sanders, Jeanne Jahnel, Susie Greene, and Charlene Hostutler; (second row) Paula Moore, Carol Jahnel, Cindy Morey, Cathy Smith, and Jan'et Greene. (Both, courtesy of Jan'et Schaef.)

Shown above is a 1947 wheat harvest in the Gem community on the Moore place. Although combine crews would come through the area on their way north to the border with Canada, the combine here was owned by the Moore brothers. (Courtesy of Walton Moore.)

The Elvin Parrotts farmed in the Gem community on land purchased from J. W. Moore in 1920. In 1967, Walton and Morris Moore purchased his grandfather's land from the Parrotts and moved his family to the homestead, shown above. Florence Craig Moore is standing in the middle wearing the ever-present apron. (Courtesy of Walton Moore.)

Walton Moore, present owner of the old Parrott house, took this photograph outside a cave on Okinawa, where he braved Typhoon Louise, not named for his wife, Louise, in October 1945. According to the Naval History Web site, "The wind shifted to the north, and then to the northwest, and began to blow ships back off the west and north reefs . . . sometimes dragging anchor the entire way." (Courtesy of Walton Moore.)

Four men from Hemphill County met in New York City prior to shipping out on the *Queen Mary* in 1945. Bill Hodges is in the passenger seat; Morris Moore is on the far right in back followed by Kenneth Riley and Horace Curnutt in the back middle. These men returned from the war, as did many like them, to make substantial contributions to the community. (Courtesy of Morris Moore.)

Henry and Lottie Jahnel came to the Gem community from Germany in 1904. Their sons Cleo and Henry are shown above in front of their newly built farmhouse in 1914. Shown below is a family picture around 1925 after their son Carl was added to the family. On the first row are Cleo, Carl, and Lottie. On the second row are Lawrence and Henry. Cleo was a recognized leader and member of the Hemphill County Wind Erosion Board, founded in 1947 and later renamed the Soil and Water Conservation Board. (Both, courtesy of Sally Jahnel Flowers.)

The Forgey ranch house (pictured above), built before 1900, was the birthplace of Oscar, son of Joseph and Jeanie Forgey. Oscar married Mabel Alexander, and they lived on the ranch near Gem City with their two daughters, Janet and Eleanor. Shown in the picture are Joe and Jeanie Forgey and their children. Cabin Creek Hereford Ranch is the result of that effort and remains in the family today.

Jim Ramp, shown above, rests his arm on a concrete water tank built by his grandfather H. M. Ramp, who came to eastern Hemphill County in 1893 to found Ramp Ranch in the Gem community. Where no natural water existed, early ranchers built a wire form and poured concrete to construct a water tank next to a windmill. This one has an autograph: "HM RAMP 5/17/09 BUILDER." (Courtesy of Rhea Wilson.)

Shown above is the interior of the Glazier Drug Store in the early 20th century. The post office for the community was located in the drugstore, a common occurrence in smaller communities like this one.

Main Street in Glazier is shown in the above photograph. J. F. Johnson, on whose ranchland the town was platted in 1887, named the town for his friend H. C. Glazier. Glazier was located north of the Canadian River and became a valuable shipping point for cattle. The population was about 300 in 1915, and in 1916, a fire destroyed much of the business district.

Shown above is an oil rig at Glazier in a photograph taken in 1931. This would be one of the earliest oil wells in Hemphill County, and a true oil boom would be decades away. Technology would have to evolve for the deeper oil and gas reserves in Hemphill County to become accessible. (Courtesy of Carolyn Welch.)

The Glazier booster station, shown above in 1931, was constructed to collect natural gas from nearby locations and then compress it. In later decades, this would be commonplace, and the oil and natural gas development in the county increased in volume. (Courtesy of Carolyn Welch.)

Bulldozing debris in piles for the loading cranes.

Shown above is an image of the damage when a tornado claimed 12 lives at Glazier on April 9, 1947. This tornado hit White Deer, Glazier, and Higgins in Texas. A total of 53 lives were lost in Glazier and Higgins. It cut a trail 1½ miles wide and traveled a total of 221 miles across parts of Texas, Oklahoma, and Kansas. Below is another photograph of the Glazier tornado damage. One emergency hospital was established at the First Methodist Church in Canadian, and the Canadian Hospital, with a seven-bed capacity, had admitted 21 patients.

Salvaging what they can. A pitiful sight thruout the storm wrecked area.

According to the *Canadian Record*, "This third great blow of a pioneer lifetime was too much for the tiny hamlet of Glazier, once one of the largest cattle shipping points in the Southwest. Twice before the town of Glazier had been destroyed by fire, and each time it has been reborn." Many residents have indicated they will not return.

Elmer Sparks came to Texas to run his parents' ranch northwest of Glazier in 1946. His stepfather, Walter Scott, and his mother, Annie, were killed in the 1947 tornado. Sparks chaired the Hemphill County Historical Committee, which had as members Polly Tubb, Lois Bryant, and Palma Morris. Sparks was named Man of the Year in 1970. Shown above is Sparks harvesting grain sorghum on the ranch. (Courtesy of Carolyn Welch.)

Shown above is the Cataline community in the early 1920s. W. A. Donaldson donated the land for the school when it was rebuilt in 1890. The white frame school is identified with two dots above it in the background. Pictured below is a group of Cataline schoolchildren. To the left of the school is Bill Donaldson's house and the Cataline Post Office, with a single dot above it. Three dots identify the Bob Knowles store. (Both, courtesy of *Hemphill County News*.)

Visit us at
arcadiapublishing.com

.

www.ingramcontent.com/pod-product-compliance
Lightning Source LLC
Chambersburg PA
CBHW050632110426
42813CB00007B/1785